# APPLICATION OF THE MICHAEL CHEKHOV TECHNIQUE TO SHAKESPEARE'S SONNETS, SOLILOQUIES, AND MONOLOGUES

*Mark Monday*

First published 2020
by Routledge
52 Vanderbilt Avenue, New York, NY 10017

and by Routledge
2 Park Square, Milton Park, Abingdon, Oxon, OX14 4RN

*Routledge is an imprint of the Taylor & Francis Group, an informa business*

© 2020 Taylor & Francis

The right of Mark Monday to be identified as author of this work has been asserted by him in accordance with sections 77 and 78 of the Copyright, Designs and Patents Act 1988.

All rights reserved. No part of this book may be reprinted or reproduced or utilised in any form or by any electronic, mechanical, or other means, now known or hereafter invented, including photocopying and recording, or in any information storage or retrieval system, without permission in writing from the publishers.

*Trademark notice*: Product or corporate names may be trademarks or registered trademarks, and are used only for identification and explanation without intent to infringe.

*Library of Congress Cataloging-in-Publication Data*
A catalog record for this book has been requested

ISBN: 978-0-367-34968-4 (hbk)
ISBN: 978-0-367-34970-7 (pbk)
ISBN: 978-0-429-32907-4 (ebk)

Typeset in New Baskerville
by Apex CoVantage, LLC
Printed and bound by CPI Group (UK) Ltd, Croydon, CR0 4YY

Visit the eResources: www.routledge.com/9780367349707

# APPLICATION OF THE MICHAEL CHEKHOV TECHNIQUE TO SHAKESPEARE'S SONNETS, SOLILOQUIES, AND MONOLOGUES

*Application of the Michael Chekhov Technique to Shakespeare's Sonnets, Soliloquies, and Monologues* illustrates how to apply the Michael Chekhov Technique, through exercises and rehearsal techniques, to a wide range of Shakespeare's works.

The book begins with a comprehensive chapter on the definitions of the various aspects of the Technique, followed by five chapters covering Shakespeare's sonnets, comedies, tragedies, histories, and romances. This volume offers a very specific path, via Michael Chekhov, on how to put theory into practice and bring one's own artistic life into the work of Shakespeare.

Offering a wide range of pieces that can be used as audition material, *Application of the Michael Chekhov Technique to Shakespeare's Sonnets, Soliloquies, and Monologues* is an excellent resource for acting teachers, directors, and actors specializing in the work of William Shakespeare.

The book also includes access to a video on Psychological Gesture to facilitate the application of this acting tool to Shakespeare's scenes.

**Mark Monday** was a Founding Director of the Great Lakes Michael Chekhov Consortium and served as its President and Producing Artistic Director. He was also a professional actor, director, and teacher.

*For*
*Cathy, Lionel, and Lavinia*

# CONTENTS

*Preface and How to Use This Book*        xiv

**Chapter One: Tools of the Michael Chekhov
                Technique Used in This Book**      1

**Chapter Two: The Sonnets**        7

*Sonnet Fourteen 'Not from the stars do I my judgment
     pluck;'   11*
*Sonnet Seventeen 'Who will believe my verse in time
     to come,'   13*
*Sonnet Twenty-Three 'As an unperfect actor on the
     stage'   15*
*Sonnet Twenty-Seven 'Weary with toil I haste me to
     my bed,'   16*
*Sonnet Thirty-Four 'Why didst thou promise such a
     beauteous day,'   17*
*Sonnet Forty-Two 'That thou hast her, it is not all my
     grief,'   18*
*Sonnet Forty-Six 'My heart doth plead that thou in him
     dost lie—'   20*
*Sonnet Fifty-Six 'Sweet love, renew thy force; be it
     not said'   22*
*Sonnet Sixty 'Like as the waves make towards the
     pebbled shore,'   23*
*Sonnet Eighty 'O, how I faint when I of you do write,'   25*
*Sonnet One Hundred-Sixteen 'Let me not to the marriage
     of true minds'   26*

viii CONTENTS

*Sonnet One Hundred-Thirty 'My mistress' eyes are nothing
like the sun;'* 28
*Sonnet One Hundred-Forty-Four 'Two loves I have of comfort
and despair,'* 29

## Chapter Three: The Comedies – Women 32

*As You Like It* 33
    Act III, sc. iv 33
    Phoebe 33
*As You Like It* 37
    Act III, sc. v 37
    Rosalind 37
*The Comedy of Errors* 40
    Act III, sc. ii 40
    Luciana 40
*The Merchant of Venice* 43
    Act III, sc. iv 43
    Portia 43
*The Merchant of Venice* 45
    Act IV, sc. i 45
    Portia 45
*A Midsummer Night's Dream* 47
    Act I, sc. i 47
    Helena 47
*A Midsummer Night's Dream* 49
    Act I, sc. i 49
    Helena 49
*A Midsummer Night's Dream* 51
    Act II, sc. i 51
    Titania 51
*Twelfth Night* 53
    Act II, sc. ii 53
    Viola 53
*Twelfth Night* 55
    Act III, sc. i 55
    Olivia 55
*The Two Gentlemen of Verona* 57
    Act I, sc. ii 57
    Julia 57
*The Two Gentlemen of Verona* 58
    Act IV, sc. iv 58
    Julia 58

CONTENTS ix

*As You Like It  61*
   Act II, sc. i  61
   Duke Senior  61
*As You Like It  63*
   Act II, sc. i  63
   First Lord  63
*Love's Labour's Lost  64*
   Act IV, sc. ii  64
   Berowne  64
*The Merchant of Venice  66*
   Act I, sc. iii  66
   Shylock  66
*The Merchant of Venice  67*
   Act II, sc. ii  67
   Launcelot Gobbo  67
*A Midsummer Night's Dream  69*
   Act I, sc. i  69
   Lysander  69
*A Midsummer Night's Dream  70*
   Act IV, sc. i  70
   Bottom  70
*Much Ado About Nothing  71*
   Act II, sc. iii  71
   Benedick  71
*Twelfth Night  73*
   Act I, sc. i  73
   Orsino  73
*The Two Gentlemen of Verona  75*
   Act II, sc. iii  75
   Launce  75

**Chapter Four: The Tragedies – Women**　　　　　**79**

*Antony and Cleopatra  79*
   Act I, sc. v  79
   Cleopatra  79
*Antony and Cleopatra  80*
   Act IV, sc. xv  80
   Cleopatra  80
*Hamlet  82*
   Act II, sc. i  82
   Ophelia  82

# CONTENTS

*Hamlet   83*
   Act III, sc. i   83
   Ophelia   83
*Hamlet   85*
   Act IV, sc. vii   85
   Gertrude   85
*Julius Caesar   86*
   Act II, sc. i   86
   Portia   86
*Julius Caesar   87*
   Act II, sc. ii   87
   Calphurnia   87
*King Lear   88*
   Act I, sc. iv   88
   Goneril   88
*Macbeth   90*
   Act I, sc. v   90
   Lady Macbeth   90
*Macbeth   91*
   Act I, sc. vii   91
   Lady Macbeth   91
*Othello   93*
   Act IV, sc. iii   93
   Emelia   93
*Romeo and Juliet   94*
   Act III, sc. ii   94
   Juliet   94
*Antony and Cleopatra   96*
   Act II, sc. ii   96
   Enobarbus   96
*Coriolanus   98*
   Act IV, sc. v   98
   Coriolanus   98
*Hamlet   100*
   Act I, sc. iii   100
   Polonius   100
*Julius Caesar   102*
   Act I, sc. ii   102
   Cassius   102
*Julius Caesar   104*
   Act II, sc. i   104
   Brutus   104

CONTENTS xi

*Julius Caesar  105*
    Act III, sc. i  105
    Antony  105
*King Lear  107*
    Act I, sc. ii  107
    Edmund  107
*Macbeth  109*
    Act I, sc. vii  109
    Macbeth  109
*Othello  110*
    Act I, sc. i  110
    Iago  110
*Romeo and Juliet  111*
    Act II, sc. ii  111
    Romeo  111
*Titus Andronicus  113*
    Act III, sc. ii  113
    Titus  113
*Titus Andronicus  115*
    Act IV, sc. ii  115
    Aaron  115

**Chapter Five: The Histories – Women**    **119**

*Richard II  119*
    Act I, sc. ii  119
    Duchess of Gloucester  119
*Henry IV, Part Two  121*
    Act II, sc. iii  121
    Lady Percy  121
*Henry V  122*
    Prologue  122
    Chorus  122
*Henry VI, Pt. 1  124*
    Act I, sc. ii  124
    Joan de Pucelle  124
*Henry VI, Pt. II  125*
    Act I, sc. iii  125
    Queen Margaret  125
*Henry Six, Pt. II  126*
    Act II, sc. iv  126
    Eleanor  126

xii CONTENTS

*Henry VI, Pt. III* 128
  Act I, sc. iv 128
  Margaret 128
*Richard III* 130
  Act I, sc. ii 130
  Lady Anne 130
*Richard II* 131
  Act II, sc. i 131
  John of Gaunt 131
*Richard II* 133
  Act III, sc. ii 133
  King Richard 133
*Richard II* 135
  Act III, sc. iii 135
  King Richard 135
*Richard II* 137
  Act IV, sc. i 137
  Bishop of Carlisle 137
*Henry IV, Pt. 1* 139
  Act I, sc. iii 139
  Hotspur 139
*Henry IV, Pt. II* 141
  Act III, sc. i 141
  King Henry IV 141
*Henry IV, Pt. II* 142
  Act IV, sc. v 142
  Prince Hal 142
*Henry V* 144
  Act I, sc. ii 144
  King Henry V 144
*Henry V* 146
  Act IV, sc. iii 146
  King Henry V 146
*Richard III* 148
  Act I, sc. i 148
  Richard 148
*Richard III* 150
  Act I, sc. ii 150
  Richard 150
*Richard III* 152
  Act II, sc. i 152
  King Edward IV 152

CONTENTS                                                    xiii

**Chapter Six: The Romances and Problem Plays – Women:**
        **Romances**                                        **156**

*Cymbeline   156*
    Act III, sc. vi   156
    Imogen   156
*The Winter's Tale   157*
    Act III, sc. ii   157
    Hermione   157
*The Winter's Tale   159*
    Act III, sc. ii   159
    Paulina   159
*Cymbeline   160*
    Act II, sc. ii   160
    Iachimo   160
*The Tempest   163*
    Act II, sc. ii   163
    Trinculo   163
*The Tempest   164*
    Act III, sc. ii   164
    Caliban   164
*The Tempest   165*
    Act IV, sc. i   165
    Prospero   165
*All's Well That Ends Well   167*
    Act III, sc. ii   167
    Helena   167
*Measure for Measure   169*
    Act II, sc. ii   169
    Isabella   169
*Troilus and Cressida   170*
    Act III, sc. ii   170
    Cressida   170
*Measure for Measure   172*
    Act III, sc. i   172
    Claudio   172

*Appendix I Exercises: Contributed by Colleagues and Teachers*
    *of the Great Lakes Michael Chekhov Consortium*        *174*
*Appendix II Practice Monologues for Identifying the Score*        *192*
*Appendix III Compilation of Notes Pertinent to All Speeches*      *199*
*Index*                                                            *202*

# PREFACE AND HOW TO USE THIS BOOK

The work of Michael Chekhov, and the study of it, continues to grow worldwide. It is thrilling to be a part of it. I began my Chekhov journey in 1978 when I bought my first copy of *To the Actor*. Coming from an athletic background, I was fascinated with the possibilities of the physicality of the exercises. I soon found out that the Chekhov Technique is near impossible to comprehend from a book—from an individual's perspective. It needs, to be properly learned, a teacher and an ensemble of actors willing to immerse themselves into the work without judgement.

Fast forward to 2001 when I had the privilege to attend my first conference with the Michael Chekhov Association (MICHA.) There I worked with Joanna Merlin and Jack Colvin—both of whom had studied with Michael Chekhov. I later worked with Mala Powers on several occasions in southern California. Mala also studied with Chekhov. These experiences proved the above—we must be present in a studio with competent teachers who can provide guidance from experience with the Technique.

With that said, I hope this book is user friendly. If you commit yourself to the challenges I propose, follow the notes I provide after each monologue or soliloquy and do the exercises in the Appendix, I believe the work will be of great value to you. If you are a teacher, using this volume for a class, I suggest you begin with the exercises on Psychological Gesture and complete all of the exercises before delving into the text. You'll find it an easier application if you proceed this way.

There always arise two questions when conversing with others about the Chekhov Technique: does the Technique work for everyone, and

## PREFACE AND HOW TO USE THIS BOOK    XV

why use it exclusively? The Technique indeed works for everyone that has, or is willing to invest in, an active imagination. I say invest in because the Technique is not only based in imagination but trains it as well. There are those, from another major methodology, who say the imagination is unreliable in consistent truthful acting. Well, this is simply not accurate. Actors work in imaginary circumstances in an elevated medium. Acting does not mimic everyday life. Everyday life is mostly filled with mundane tasks, home life, and work-related events. Occasionally, a major event occurs, and we deal with those circumstances according to our own nature, society, and culture. Not so in our world of theater. An evening of theater is elevated above any normal everyday existence and requires us, actors and audience, to engage our imagination—our fantasy lives. I further propose there is much more detail to the Chekhov Technique than any other. Therefore, and again if the actor is willing to take the imaginative leap, there is plenty in the Technique for everyone. If not keen on Qualities of Movement, there is Sensations. The list is comprehensive. One more thing—there is no other methodology that addresses character and characterization as comprehensively as Chekhov's Technique.

Then there is the matter of using the Technique exclusively—as opposed to combining Chekhov with other methodologists. The short answer is it has taken me many years of study to master the Technique. I'm still learning more about it every day. After all, 'we learn more and more about less and less.' You may think there must be a shorter path as you need to have the Technique work for you immediately. There is no other technique that you can apply to text immediately upon learning it. You can do an exercise in Imaginary Body, for instance, and you will know how to implement it. It is also a technique that we can use text to learn the exercises. Other techniques have the actor(s) do an exercise, but it doesn't seem to have an immediate application. I have studied Stanislavski, Hagen, Adler, and some Meisner, and none is as immediate applicable to text as is Michael Chekhov. By the way, of the major methodologists only Chekhov worked with Stanislavski. Stanislavski referred to Chekhov as his 'most brilliant pupil.' Chekhov deeply respected Stanislavski and encourages us to study especially analysis as proposed by him.

In our training environs, unless a student is in a true conservatory, acting classes are taught in the curriculum just as any other class—on

xvi PREFACE AND HOW TO USE THIS BOOK

a two day per week schedule. I encourage the reader to do the math. There is precious little time, less than five hours per semester, for individual students. It's a tragic scenario that we pretend to train actors in these circumstances. I was lucky enough to have attended a major conservatory where we had acting, movement, and voice classes every day from 11 a.m. to 5 p.m. with rehearsals beginning at 7 p.m. Our 'academic' classes began at 8 a.m. and ended at 10:45 a.m. Acting training in a liberal arts curriculum is vastly different.

Most acting teachers in liberal arts schools teach a very wide eclectic palate as concerns technique. Well, unfortunately teaching eclectically offers little technique at all. Even if you, as a teacher or actor, disagree with this proposal the best you can say is that it is 'my own' technique—one that works for me. For you have taken a pinch of this and that and somehow molded it into a process that does not necessarily work for another actor. It just makes sense to me to concentrate on one specific technique that is proven to work for most and encourage students to seek further study in the technique beyond the academy.

Dancers and musicians study specific techniques and practice those techniques for a lifetime. Most actors don't practice at all after the academy. That's because they haven't learned how to practice. The Chekhov Technique provides us with a multitude of exercises that we can practice. Chekhov says, 'repetition is the growing power.' With Chekhov we have a beautiful Technique we can practice and repeat for a lifetime.

So—this book is meant for the actor and the teacher. To use it as intended you will need to follow some direction. At the onset the work in the book looks somewhat formulaic. The Chekhov Technique is far from that. It is the most organic way to work I have encountered. If you look at the work as a formula, you'll fall into a serious acting trap and find it difficult to dig out of. Here is the 'formula' you will encounter in the book:

PG/AC = Psychological Gesture—I Open/I Rejoice (as examples)
QA = Quality of Action—Joyfully
BP = Baptism—The Right Path
OB = Objective—I want to be successful in my career.
AM = Atmosphere—Glad/Joyful
OS = Obstacle—I'm brand new to this Technique.

## PREFACE AND HOW TO USE THIS BOOK          xvii

CX = Climax—Auxiliary or Major
ST = Stakes—The Technique will lead me to 'Inspired Acting!'

The above 'formula,' or what I'd rather refer to as the journey, to Inspired Acting, must be discovered organically—on your feet immersing yourselves in the exercises in Appendix I. You will see in all of the sonnets, monologues, and soliloquies that I might have completed the work seemingly for you. Quite the contrary. I didn't skip steps in the work. I worked on my feet and discovered each and every aspect in my scoring. Then, I did a spy-back. What did I discover? How can I label this particular aspect? When I could answer I would write it down. When I couldn't answer, I rehearsed it again. Once you find the answer in an organic and physical way, you'll be able to repeat it. If you simply sit at Starbucks or your favorite bar writing down what you think the answers should be, you'll find that it's devoid of feeling. Working in a physical way (form) leads you to a psychological experience. It doesn't work in the reverse. Yes, it's a lot of work in the beginning. As you progress the work becomes much faster.

Now, back to the work in the book. It is a good start if you can work through the speeches as suggested by my 'journey.' It is not the way you will ultimately work but when learning the Technique, you may find it helpful. Afterward, you can score your own journey—and I insist on that. Finding your own journey is the only way you'll experience a true psycho-physical process. You won't experience it so much by copying my journey. You will, however, learn how the process can proceed.

As you are working on the speeches please don't discriminate by gender. Work through all the speeches and especially look at the notes after each. In fact, it is probably a good idea to look at the notes first and then work through. As I was writing I noticed that many notes apply to all speeches so don't neglect them. In Chapter 1, you'll encounter an outline of how to rehearse. This is where repetition comes in. Learn first 'how' to rehearse by working on one sonnet until it becomes second nature to you. This is the beginning, the foundation, of your own journey in the Technique. Build a strong foundation, and the rest will be strong as well.

There are some things this book isn't. It isn't a book that includes scansion, voice, or a comprehensive guide of the given circumstances. Had I illuminated those things for you the book would be the size of Webster's dictionary. I mean for the work in this book to complement

xviii     PREFACE AND HOW TO USE THIS BOOK

all of the above. Here are some books I would suggest if you are serious about studying Shakespeare as there is no one book that covers everything:

*To the Actor* by Michael Chekhov
Note: Many exercises in the Appendix are additional to those that appear in *To the Actor*.

*The Riverside Shakespeare* (complete works)
*Shakespeare's Words—A Glossary & Language Companion* by David Crystal and Ben Crystal
*Speak the Speech—Shakespeare's Monologues Illuminated* by Rhona Silverbush and Sami Plotkin
Note: *Speak the Speech—Shakespeare's Monologues Illuminated* is a must-have to accompany my book. I am a great admirer of Silverbush and Plotkin's work.

*Shakespeare's Sonnets—The Arden Shakespeare* edited by Katherine Duncan-Jones
*The Shakespeare Workbook and Video* by David Carey and Rebecca Clark Carey

You can get all of these books on Amazon for less than $100.00— an incredible investment for your career. Again, *Speak the Speech— Shakespeare's Monologues Illuminated* is the book that is most important to accompany mine.

I'd like to get back around to something I mentioned earlier in this Preface and that is 'Inspired Acting' because that is what we all are attempting to achieve. It is the place in which the job and craft of acting becomes a work of art. Rest assured there are actors who are craftspersons and there are actors who are artists. Which would you prefer?

Inspired Acting happens when an actor is properly working the tools in the Technique from a place Michael Chekhov calls the 'Higher Ego.' The Higher Ego is that place where we are only concentrating on the imaginary given circumstances at hand. Our everyday life is left behind, and we are acting (behaving) moment-to-moment. It is the place where we are intently listening and reacting in a truthful manner in accordance with the given circumstances of the play. If you work

## PREFACE AND HOW TO USE THIS BOOK                xix

properly within the various aspects of the Technique, you will find your Higher Ego. It takes investing wholeheartedly in your imagination and committing to the journey you find in the scoring of your role.

If you want to begin or continue your journey in the Michael Chekhov Technique, please consider joining us at Great Lakes Michael Chekhov Consortium (GLMCC.) We offer certification programs in acting and teaching. If you join GLMCC you'll join a family of actors and teachers worldwide. We are dedicated to realizing Chekhov's dream of 'Ideal Theater.' It will be a theater that celebrates and doesn't exploit the actor. Please visit: greatlakesmichaelchekhovconsortium.com or simply search for GLMCC. Should you have any questions about our organization or wish to ask questions about the contents in this book you can contact me directly via GLMCC's website. I'm always happy to talk about the work of Michael Chekhov!

# Chapter One

# TOOLS OF THE MICHAEL CHEKHOV TECHNIQUE USED IN THIS BOOK

**You will find in Appendix I more terminology with expanded definitions and exercises on much of the following:**

## Accents (AX)

A spike in atmosphere. You'll see I deal with AX's for a brief while and then allow you to deal with them on your own. This will make sense as you work through the book.

## Action (AC)

Action can be defined as (*what I do to get what I want*). Actions are discovered through the given circumstances. They are verbs such as: I smash, I embrace, I penetrate, I lift. They are what we do to reach our goals. I strongly prefer that actors begin with 'I' to state their AC's. The actor is playing the character. The character is not playing the actor.

**Note: You will work with industry professionals who use the word 'tactics' instead of Action. Simply know that what they really mean is Action as a tactic is something we plan to do. Once we put the plan into motion it becomes Action. (Drives me nuts.)**

## Archetype (AR)

Every character, every human being, is composed of various archetypes. I write about this extensively in my first book, *Directing with the Michael Chekhov Technique*. For our purposes in this volume I identify characters with archetypes in each soliloquy or monologue.

2    TOOLS OF THE TECHNIQUE USED IN THIS BOOK

AR's are universal truths that identify and categorize us. They guide actors in choices of AC's and Qualities of Action. AR's serve us in how the audience knows the characters.

A good source for archetype definitions is 'Archetype Cards' by Caroline Myss. The cards are available on Amazon—as is my first book.

## Artistic Frame (AF)

The Artistic Frame is similar to, yet more profound, than Stanislavski's 'beats.' Stanislavski describes the beat as 'one swing of the pendulum.' That is a lovely image. The AF has a beginning, middle, and ending. Lenard Petit says it is 'preparation, sustaining and radiating.' In our organization, the Great Lakes Michael Chekhov Consortium, we have labeled the AF with Fantasize, Do, Radiate (FDR). It really is all of these things that make it profound.

When using FDR we first fantasize the AC (the Psychological Gesture, PG, see below) and the Quality of Action (also see below) preceding the physical body toward our scene partner. It is not necessarily a visual image we are fantasizing. Rather, we fantasize the feeling of our OB being fulfilled because our AC and Quality of Action are successful. We get what we want and we feel great about it—we feel glad. Chekhov teaches us to 'see our objective fulfilled' before we execute the Action. To fantasize first, adheres to this directive.

After fantasizing the objective fulfilled and we are full of joy (glad) we then follow the fantasy with the physical doing of the AC and Quality of Action. Afterward we sustain or radiate the feeling until we begin to sense it dissipating. Eventually we recognize a clear ending and move onto the next AF—a new beginning. It is crucial to make the ending clear so we move, and we move the audience, from frame to frame and thereby make the story of the play crystal clear.

Chekhov teaches us to say when working on form, 'Now I begin my movement which creates a form.' Upon completion of the form he says, 'Now I finished it; the form is there.' When you are rehearsing using a form, a Psychological Gesture, it's a good practice to use these phrases.

Please note we are not playing a feeling or emotion. We are instead fantasizing an atmosphere that we have experienced hundreds of times. Those archetypal atmospheres are stored in our bodies and we can coax them forward via our imagination—our fantasy life.

# TOOLS OF THE TECHNIQUE USED IN THIS BOOK 3

## [A] Atmosphere (AM)

Chekhov describes AM's as, 'the source of ineffable moods and waves of feeling that emanate from one's own surroundings.' This description is somewhat not useful to actors and directors because we must be able to articulate the AM's of the play. Yet, to respect Chekhov's words, we understand that AM's live in the realm of emotion and there are times when emotions are difficult to express. Then, there is our knowledge that emotions cannot be played. Emotions must be coaxed into existence via the playing of AC's and Qualities of Action.

So, are we on a slippery slope? Not at all. We simply must acknowledge that AM's are written into the given circumstances of the play and then conduct our behavior within those AM's accordingly. We behave differently in the AM of Fear than we do in the AM of Happiness.

AM's can be anything we recognize in the realm of mood. There could be an AM of anger or of reverence, of sadness or of a circus. Think of the AM of a church that is hundreds of years old and how one's mood might be altered upon entering. Chekhov often works with archetypes or things that are universally recognized such as Psychological Gesture and Qualities of Movement. While he doesn't give us specific archetypes for AM we can borrow from the world of psychology the following: mad, glad, sad, bad, and fear. Psychologists tell us that these five emotions are all encompassing, and all other emotions can be categorized into one of the words in this list. I have found this useful in beginning work. We can get more specific as our work progresses—if we need to do so.

There are two kinds of AM in our Technique: Objective and Individual Feelings. The Objective AM belongs to the space in which we occupy: a cathedral, rock concert, funeral, birthday party. Individual Feelings is the mood we are in at any given time. One might be in a happy mood walking down a tree-lined street. That mood changes quickly should one witness a horrific accident. Still, one might be in a happy mood at a funeral. It all depends on the given circumstances.

Finally, Chekhov points out that two conflicting AM's cannot exist for an indefinite period of time. Eventually, one AM will give way to another. This occurs when someone acquiesces or leaves the stage. Regardless, AM helps the actor and director create conflict—something that is imperative in our work.

# 4 TOOLS OF THE TECHNIQUE USED IN THIS BOOK

## Baptism (BP)

The name, or title, of an AF. When working on speeches it is useful to title each AF with a specific description. We always begin with 'The'. The Confrontation, The Game, The Conclusion, as an example. This will be clear when we begin looking at speeches.

## Composition

A series of 'laws' as described by Chekhov in his book, *To the Actor*. Some of these laws we can use in our study of sonnets, soliloquies, and monologues. (See Appendix I.)

**Climaxes (CX)**—While it is seemingly obvious that climaxes exist it is prudent to mention them because of the way in which Chekhov suggests we rehearse. It is not the traditional beginning to end process. He suggests we begin rehearsing with the climaxes first and although he means in the context of an entire play, I have found that rehearsing this way in speeches works equally as well. When working on the speeches you'll need to discover the climaxes. Once you discover the main climax, rehearse it first until you feel the height of it. Then, you can return to the beginning to build your Rhythmical Wave. (See below.)

**Inner/Outer Tempo**—There are times when our inner tempo is quite different than our outer tempo, and it is very interesting to witness on the stage. Imagine trying desperately to hold your temper. Your inner tempo is raging while your outer tempo is fighting to slow things down. It works the other way as well. Imagine an athlete who is spending a tremendous amount of energy (outer tempo) while his or her inner tempo is calm. We tend to call this 'being in the zone.' The great tennis player Roger Federer is a prime example of this. He is always in control of his inner tempo.

## Method of Psycho-Physical Action

*Action—Objective—Obstacles—Quality of Action—Stakes*

### Action (AC)

See definition above.

# TOOLS OF THE TECHNIQUE USED IN THIS BOOK        5

### *Objective (OB)*

The character's immediate goal. The definition of OB is (*what I want*).

### *Obstacles (OS)*

The definition of OS is (*what is in the way of what I want*).

### *Quality of Action (QA)*

As I have said the AC is a verb. The QA is then an adverb. I embrace—
tenderly. I penetrate—forcefully. I lift—carefully. Again, all of this
depends on the given circumstances. The definition of QA is (*how I do
what I do to get what I want*).

### *Stakes (ST)*

Literally, what is at stake. The definition of stakes is (*what I stand to lose
if I don't get what I want*). It could also be stated (*what I stand to gain if I
get what I want*). I find it depends on the given circumstances and the
archetype of the character as to which definition best suits.

    **Polarity (PL)**—As Chekhov notes, in a well-written play there is a
transformation from the beginning to the ending. As in *Midsummer* it is
a transformation from evil (anger) to good or joy (glad). This is a good
'law of composition' to incorporate in our work in this book for it adds
great variety and creates a journey for the character. Chekhov states,
'All the main qualities of the first section should transform themselves
into their opposites in the last section.'

    For our purposes we also look for Polarity in our AC's and Quali-
ties of Action. If 'I smash' as our AC is not working to accomplish our
objective, we may choose to change to 'I embrace.' We begin to build
a Rhythmical Wave in this way and take our audience on a beautiful
journey.

## Psychological Gesture (PG)

Our work in this book on PG will be mainly concerned with it as
Action. The PG's we will explore are: Open, Close, Push, Pull, Lift,

# 6 TOOLS OF THE TECHNIQUE USED IN THIS BOOK

Embrace, Throw, Tear (Rip), Wring, Penetrate, and Smash. These PG's as Actions are archetypal—meaning they serve as physical forms that are completely recognizable. Each PG has a specific form. You can find a video of actors demonstrating the forms of the PG's at www.routledge.com/9780367349707

**Note: It is a very good idea to look up the definitions for the 11 PG's and write them down. You'll find a description of how to rehearse the PG's and QA's in Chapter 2.**

Like AM's, these words are all encompassing. All Actions will fall into one of these PGs. We can therefore begin with these words in our process and get more specific, if necessary, as we move on.

The PG has two parts. In the beginning, when just working on the form of the PG, it is called an Archetypal Gesture. It becomes a PG when we add a QA. We say our work is psycho-physical. It may be helpful to think of it as physical-psycho. At first the work is physical—it is manifested as a form—an Action. When we add the QA it then transforms into the psychological.

Chekhov says that the PG can be used for other purposes. It can be used as a form for the overall character, for a scene, monologue, a line, or a single word. The PG is the one aspect of the Technique that many actors and teachers have heard of. It may also be widely misunderstood.

**Rhythmical Wave (RW)**—The journey created, like a roller coaster, by adhering to the other laws. The RW also includes tempo and rhythm.

**End Chapter One**

# Chapter Two

# THE SONNETS

I suppose a question to be asked is, why include sonnets in this book? It is my belief that working on sonnets as soliloquies is an important first step for actors. I also believe the sonnets are audition worthy material. It certainly opens up a plethora of material for women who need classic audition pieces. With that said, I always tell my female students not to avoid male speeches. Cross gender casting in Shakespeare happens often—as it should.

Hopefully, you will see the worth of working on sonnets immediately. At the least you can get a sense of how this book will aid in your teaching or performing by looking at the sonnet structure and template first as we are only dealing with 14 lines.

There is another huge plus for working on sonnets. There are no existing circumstances concerning character and characterization. You are therefore free to create a character from scratch using techniques in the book. You can certainly begin with the AR of Poet as it will be germane to all sonnets. Why not try the AR's of Poet and Soldier? Be bold!

Finally, experiment with varying tempo/rhythm in each AF. No two frames should be alike in that regard. Generally, actors tend to speak Shakespeare (especially sonnets) too fast and without variances in tempo/rhythm.

### Review of Abbreviations

AC = Action
AR = Archetype
AF = Artistic Frame

8 THE SONNETS

AM = Atmosphere
BP = Baptism
AX = Accent
CX = Climaxes
PL = Polarity
RW = Rhythmical Wave
OB = Objective
QA = Quality of Action
OS = Obstacle
ST = Stakes
PG = Psychological Gesture

**Review of PG's**

Open
Close
Pull
Push
Embrace
Wring
Throw
Tear (Rip)
Penetrate
Lift
Smash

**Note that each AF is bracketed []**

## Sonnet One

### *AF 1*

PG/AC = I Open (I Instruct)
QA = Excitedly
BP = The Declaration
OB = I want him/her/they/them to procreate!
AM = Glad
OS = Stubbornness of the listener
CX = Major

# THE SONNETS

ST = This is where the actor can begin to think about character. She or he can make the stakes as high as they wish. What if the speaker wants desperately to sleep with the listener? So, ST = The loss of making love with this person.

Here is the process concerning how to rehearse sonnets and all other speeches contained in the book:

1. Imagine the AM of Glad. (**See Atmosphere exercise in Appendix I.**)
2. Execute the form of the PG of AF 1, 3X. While standing in a place of readiness breathe in. Execute the PG and exhale. Incorporate your imagination as described in Chapter 1 and in Appendix I.
3. Execute the form of the PG. Just at the finish say the words, 'I Open' 3X.
   **Note: For this rehearsal/exercise come back to a place of readiness after each.**
4. Execute the form of the PG. Just at the finish say the words, 'I Instruct' 3X.
5. Execute the form of the PG. Just at the finish say the words, 'I Instruct' and add the QA of Excitedly. 3X. Invest in the QA of Excitedly both physically and vocally.
6. Execute the form of the PG. Just at the finish say the words, 'The Declaration.' It is important to say 'The Declaration' with the quality of declaring. 3X.
7. Execute the form of the PG. Just at the finish say the words, 'The Declaration' and continue with the text. Drive the AC and QA throughout AF 1. 3X.
8. When you feel you have committed to the work 100% move onto AF 2. When you feel you have committed 100% to AF 2 go back and put AF's 1 and 2 together. When you feel you have committed 100% to 1 and 2, begin work on AF 3. All steps 3X.
9. When you feel you have committed 100% to AF 3 go back and put the entire speech together.
10. Never skip steps. This is the actor's homework. With proper rehearsal the speech will be engrained in your physical being. It will be organic and completely repeatable.
11. Eventually, do not come back to a place of readiness after each. Instead, hold your form in each AF moving from one form to the next.

## 10                                  THE SONNETS

**Note: In this first sonnet I have indicated my choices of operative words by underlining them. It's the only time I will do this. These are my choices. Operative words should be limited to two or three (at most) in each line. If you can speak only the operative words in each line and make some sense of the sonnet, you will know you have chosen the correct words.**

[From fairest creatures we desire increase,
That thereby beauty's rose might never die,
But as the riper should by time decease,
His tender heir might bear his memory:] *End AF 1*

### *AF 2*

PG/AC = I Close (PL from I Open-helping create a RW) (I Chide)
QA = Sternly
BP = The Truth
OB = Same as AF 1
AM = Mad
OS = Same as AF 1
CX = Auxiliary
ST = Same as AF 1

[But thou, contracted to thine own bright eyes,
Feed'st thy light'st flame with self-substantial fuel,
Making a famine where abundance lies,
Thyself thy foe, to thy sweet self too cruel.] *End AF 2*

**Note: Have a look at an alternate way of doing *AF 2*. I encourage you to do this throughout your work in this book and throughout your career!**

### *AF 2 Alternate*

PG/AC = I Close (PL from I Open-helping create a RW) (I Chide)
QA = Sorrowfully
BP = The Truth
OB = Same as *AF 1*
AM = Sad

THE SONNETS 11

OS = Same as *AF 1*
CX = Auxiliary
ST = Same as *AF 1*

[But thou, contracted to thine own bright eyes,
Feed'st thy light'st flame with self-substantial fuel,
Making a famine where abundance lies,
Thyself thy foe, to thy sweet self too cruel.] *End AF 2*

### *AF 3*

PG/AC = I Embrace (I Warn)
QA = Reasonably
BP = The Bottom Line
OB = Same
AM = Fear
OS = Same
CX = Major
ST = Same

[Thou that art now the world's fresh ornament
And only herald to the gaudy spring,
Within thine own bud buriest thy content
And, tender churl, makest waste in niggarding.
Pity the world, or else this glutton be,
To eat the world's due, by the grave and thee.] *End AF 3*

## Sonnet Fourteen

### *AF 1*

PG/AC = I Lift (I Reveal)
QA = Flatteringly
BP = The Tease
OB = I want him/her to take responsibility for her role in life.
AM = Glad (Hope)
OS = Denial
CX = Auxiliary

ST = Perhaps the listener is a person of rank—even the King or Queen who is not living up to their potential. The speaker then must be careful with the words so as not to offend.

[Not from the stars do I my judgment pluck;
And yet methinks I have astronomy,
But not to tell of good or evil luck,
Of plagues, of dearths, or seasons' quality;
Nor can I fortune to brief minutes tell,
Pointing to each his thunder, rain and wind,
Or say with princes if it shall go well,
By oft predict that I in heaven find:] *End AF 1*

### *AF 2*

PG/AC = I Embrace (I Share)
QA = Lovingly
BP = The Truth
OB = Same
AM = Same
OS = Same
CX = Major
ST = Same

[But from thine eyes my knowledge I derive,
And, constant stars, in them I read such art
As truth and beauty shall together thrive,
If from thyself to store thou wouldst convert;] *End AF 2*

### *AF 3*

PG/AC = I Open (I Reveal)
QA = Warningly
BP = The Fact
OB = Same

# THE SONNETS                                    13

AM = Same
OS = Same
CX = Auxiliary
ST = Same

[Or else of thee this I prognosticate:
Thy end is truth's and beauty's doom and date.] *End AF 3*

**Note: This sonnet differs in format from the first in that there is an added
AF on the rhyming couplet. This creates a dynamic Rhythmical Wave. It
is also a sonnet concerning procreation. Please feel free to adjust the
'score,' as I suggested in the Preface, to more reflect the poet's intent.**

## Sonnet Seventeen

### *AF 1*

PG/AC = I Open (I Invite)
QA = Unquestionably or Duh'ly
BP = The Challenge
OB = I want him/her to admit and declare her beauty and have
    children!
AM = Glad
OS = Stubbornness
CX = Auxiliary
ST = The poet does not live on through his or her words unless the
    listener procreates.

[Who will believe my verse in time to come,
If it were fill'd with your most high deserts?

**Note: There is an AC and a QA change here to: I Close, Exasperatedly,
helping to create Polarity and a RW. There is also an AM change to Sad.
All in only two lines!**

Though yet, heaven knows, it is but as a tomb
Which hides your life and shows not half your parts.] *End AF 1*

# THE SONNETS

## *AF 2*

PG/AC = I Embrace (I Share)
QA = Reasonably
BP = Same
OB = Same
AM = Sad
OS = Stubbornness
CX = Major (with a steady build in Tempo/Rhythm)
ST = The poet does not live on through his or her words unless the
    listener procreates.

[If I could write the beauty of your eyes
And in fresh numbers number all your graces,
The age to come would say 'This poet lies:
Such heavenly touches ne'er touch'd earthly faces.'

**Note: There is an AX—a definite spike in AM. You may also choose to
change AC and/or QA in these four lines.**

So should my papers yellow'd with their age
Be scorn'd like old men of less truth than tongue,
And your true rights be term'd a poet's rage
And stretched metre of an antique song:] *End AF 2*

## *AF 3*

PG/AC = I Penetrate (I Beg)
QA = Desperately
BP = The Plea
OB = I want him/her to admit and declare her beauty and have
    children!
AM = Glad (Hope)
OS = Stubbornness
CX = Major
ST = Same

[But were some child of yours alive that time,
You should live twice; in it and in my rhyme.] *End AF 3*

# THE SONNETS

## Sonnet Twenty-Three

### *AF 1*

PG/AC = I Wring (I Extricate)
QA = Frustratedly
BP = The Wrestling
OB = I want him or her to see the reality of my love in my words.
AM = Mad
OS = The speaker's inability to articulate what he or she wishes to say.
CX = Major
ST = He or she may lose the love of her life.

[As an unperfect actor on the stage
Who with his fear is put besides his part,
Or some fierce thing replete with too much rage,
Whose strength's abundance weakens his own heart.
So I, for fear of trust, forget to say
The perfect ceremony of love's rite,
And in mine own love's strength seem to decay,
O'ercharged with burden of mine own love's might.] *End AF 1*

### *AF 2*

PG/AC = I Pull (I Beg)
QA = Pleadingly
BP = The Proposal
OB = Same
AM = Glad (Hope)
OS = Same
CX = Auxiliary
ST = Same

[O, let my books be then the eloquence
And dumb presagers of my speaking breast,
Who plead for love and look for recompense
More than that tongue that more hath more express'd.

**Note: There should be an AC in the rhyming couplet. Accents can be treated with up or down inflection or with variance in volume.**

O, learn to read what silent love hath writ:
To hear with eyes belongs to love's fine wit.] *End AF2*

## Sonnet Twenty-Seven

### *AF 1*

PG/AC = I Push (I Press On)
QA = Difficultly
BP = The Struggle
OB = I want to rest so that my mind can contemplate (fantasize) on you!
AM = Bad
OS = So many things to do before I can retire.
CX = Auxiliary
ST = Perhaps the speaker has a rendezvous with his or her lover tomorrow.

[Weary with toil I haste me to my bed,
The dear repose for limbs with travel tired;
But then begins a journey in my head,
To work my mind, when body's work's expired:] *End AF 1*

### *AF 2*

PG/AC = I Embrace (I Capture)
QA = Dreamily
BP = The Fantasy
OB = I want to make love to him or her.
AM = Glad (Horny)
OS = He or she is so far away it makes me crazy!
CX = Major with a slow build and AC on the couplet.
ST = I'm lost if he or she does not share my fantasy.

[For then my thoughts, from far where I abide,
Intend a zealous pilgrimage to thee,

# THE SONNETS

And keep my drooping eyelids open wide,
Looking on darkness which the blind do see
Save that my soul's imaginary sight
Presents thy shadow to my sightless view,
Which, like a jewel hung in ghastly night,
Makes black night beauteous and her old face new.

**Note: You can easily give the rhyming couplet its own AF. Also consider an AC on (Lo!)**

Lo! thus, by day my limbs, by night my mind,
For thee and for myself no quiet find.] *End AF 2*

**Note: The Michael Chekhov Technique engages the Imagination from many different angles through his exercises. Hopefully you are beginning to see that, just as in singing, the performer must master the Technique and internalize the work. Only then can the imagination be truly used to create 'Inspired Acting.' What are you fantasizing when you speak sonnet twenty-seven? You perhaps should be fantasizing making love to the person you are speaking about and not paying attention to the Technique. This will work for you if you are rehearsing in the proper way.**

## Sonnet Thirty-Four

### *AF 1*

PG/AC = I Tear (I Accuse)
QA = Heatedly
BP = The Betrayal
OB = I want he or she to realize her behavior toward me and
    amend it.
AM = Mad
OS = She is set in her ways.
CX = Major
ST = Her behavior is killing me!

[Why didst thou promise such a beauteous day,
And make me travel forth without my cloak,

18        THE SONNETS

To let base clouds o'ertake me in my way,
Hiding thy bravery in their rotten smoke?
'Tis not enough that through the cloud thou break,
To dry the rain on my storm-beaten face,
For no man well of such a salve can speak
That heals the wound and cures not the disgrace:
Nor can thy shame give physic to my grief;
Though thou repent, yet I have still the loss:
The offender's sorrow lends but weak relief
To him that bears the strong offence's cross.] *End AF 1*

## *AF 2*

PG/AC = I Embrace (I Hug tightly)
QA = Ecstatically
BP = The 'But When You're Hot—You're Hot' (an exception to
    the 2–3 word rule)
OB = Same
AM = Glad
OS = Same
CX = Auxiliary
ST = Same

[Ah! but those tears are pearl which thy love sheds,
And they are rich and ransom all ill deeds.] *End AF 2*

**Note: I am introducing a couple of new things in PG/AC and BP. We
are working in an art form that only is bound by our imagination.
Don't necessarily always stick to 'the rules.' The actor's work should
be private. You can phrase a BP in any way that works for you. I like to
keep them simple because I believe in conciseness. The less we have to
articulate in our scoring the better.**

## Sonnet Forty-Two

### *AF 1*

PG/AC = I Close (I Yield)
QA = Searchingly

# THE SONNETS

BP = The Contemplation
OB = I want an answer.
AM = Sad
OS = Both loves are lost. Can there be consolation?
CX = Auxiliary
ST = I may die from grief.

[That thou hast her, it is not all my grief,
And yet it may be said I loved her dearly;
That she hath thee, is of my wailing chief,
A loss in love that touches me more nearly.] *End AF 1*

## *AF 2*

PG/AC = I Open (I Forgive)
QA = Toughly (as in difficult to give in)
BP = The Gift
OB = Same
AM = Glad (Hope)
OS = I'm doomed if they don't accept.
CX = Auxiliary
ST = Same

[Loving offenders, thus I will excuse ye:] *End AF 2*

## *AF 3*

PG/AC = I Throw (I Toss this out at you)
QA = Reasonably
BP = The Argument (as in the thesis)
OB = Same
AM = Fear
OS = Same
CX = Major
ST = Same

[Thou dost love her, because thou knowst I love her;
And for my sake even so doth she abuse me,
Suffering my friend for my sake to approve her.

# THE SONNETS

If I lose thee, my loss is my love's gain,
And losing her, my friend hath found that loss;
Both find each other, and I lose both twain,
And both for my sake lay on me this cross:] *End AF 3*

## *AF 4*

PG/AC = I Open (I Rejoice)
QA = Over-the-moonly
BP = The Answer
OB = I want to celebrate.
AM = Glad (Joy)
OS = None—Free
CX = Major with an AC
ST = The burden has been lifted!

[But here's the joy; my friend and I are one;
Sweet flattery! then she loves but me alone.] *End AF 4*

**Note: I am pushing the envelope with the number of AF's in this sonnet. Yet, we must continue to test the template to understand our parameters.**

## Sonnet Forty-Six

### *AF 1*

PG/AC = I Push—as in reacting backwards (I Jump)
QA = Surprisingly
BP = The Confusion
OB = I want to sort out my feelings
AM = Fear (There are many levels of fear)
OS = This person is so beautiful I'm at odds with my feelings and
    what I am imagining!
CX = Major
ST = This could be the person of my dreams!

[Mine eye and heart are at a mortal war
How to divide the conquest of thy sight;

# THE SONNETS

Mine eye my heart thy picture's sight would bar,
My heart mine eye the freedom of that right.] *End AF 1*

## *AF 2*

PG/AC = I Pull (I Extract)
QA = Questioningly
BP = Same
OB = Same
AM = Same
OS = Same
CX = Auxiliary
ST = Same

[My heart doth plead that thou in him dost lie—
A closet never pierced with crystal eyes—

**Note: There is a QA change (possibly) on-the-other-handly**

But the defendant doth that plea deny
And says in him thy fair appearance lies.] *End AF 2*

## *AF 3*

PG/AC = I Close (I Conclude)
QA = Decidedly
BP = The Conclusion
OB = Same
AM = Same
OS = Is my conclusion correct? If not, I may lose the person of my
    dreams.
CX = Major
ST = Same

[To 'cide this title is impaneled
A quest of thoughts, all tenants to the heart,
And by their verdict is determined
The clear eye's moiety and the dear heart's part:

22      THE SONNETS

As thus; mine eye's due is thy outward part,
And my heart's right thy inward love of heart.] *End AF 3*

## Sonnet Fifty-Six

### *AF 1*

PG/AC = I Embrace (I Advise)
QA = Lovingly
BP = The Plea.
OB = I want to help he or her to heal.
AM = Glad (for the future)
OS = The listener has lost his or her true love and is in pain.
CX = Auxiliary
ST = My pain is his or her pain. When they heal so do I.

[Sweet love, renew thy force; be it not said
Thy edge should blunter be than appetite,
Which but to-day by feeding is allay'd,
To-morrow sharpen'd in his former might:] *End AF 1*

**Note: The PG of Smash. How slowly and carefully can one Smash?
Slowly is the tempo of Caution. Also, when you research the meaning
of this sonnet be aware that you will likely encounter a scholarly point
of view. That view is not necessarily a good one for the actor. We have
to personalize the poetry and make it immediately active.**

### *AF 2*

PG/AC = I Smash (I Caution)
QA = Carefully
BP = The Tutoring
OB = Same
AM = Same
OS = Same
CX = Major
ST = Same

# THE SONNETS

[So, love, be thou; although to-day thou fill
Thy hungry eyes even till they wink with fullness,
To-morrow see again, and do not kill
The spirit of love with a perpetual dullness.] *End AF 2*

### *AF 3*

PG/AC = I Open (I Reveal—the truth)
QA = Earnestly
BP = The Gospel
OB = Same
AM = Same
OS = Same
CX = Major
ST = Same

[Let this sad interim like the ocean be
Which parts the shore, where two contracted new
Come daily to the banks, that, when they see
Return of love, more blest may be the view;
Else call it winter, which being full of care
Makes summer's welcome thrice more wish'd, more rare.] *End AF 3*

## Sonnet Sixty

**Note: This is one of the contemplative sonnets. Take care to make it active by striving to solve the problem proposed in the first quatrain. There is never an inward search on the stage. There is always 'the other' even if not present. The sonnets and soliloquies involve the audience. Have the audience help in the solving and you'll be on the proper path.**

### *AF 1*

PG/AC = I Penetrate (I Search—inside)
QA = Contemplatively
BP = The Realization
OB = I want to come to terms with the inevitable—expiration.

AM = Sad

OS = This is an age-old problem that few have answered.

CX = Auxiliary

ST = If I can't find an answer, I'll be miserable for the remainder
of my time.


[Like as the waves make towards the pebbled shore,
So do our minutes hasten to their end;
Each changing place with that which goes before,
In sequent toil all forwards do contend.] *End AF 1*


### AF 2

PG/AC = I Open (I Receive)

QA = Understandingly (I am beginning to understand slowly.)

BP = Same

OB = Same

AM = Glad (transitioning toward Glad slowly)

OS = Same

CX = Auxiliary with an AX

ST = Same


[Nativity, once in the main of light,
Crawls to maturity, wherewith being crown'd,
Crooked elipses 'gainst his glory fight,
And Time that gave doth now his gift confound.
Time doth transfix the flourish set on youth
And delves the parallels in beauty's brow,
Feeds on the rarities of nature's truth,
And nothing stands but for his scythe to mow:] *End AF 2*


### AF 3

PG/AC = I Open (I Rejoice)

QA = Joyfully

BP = The Answer

OB = Same

AM = Glad (Joy)

OS = Free

THE SONNETS                    25

CX = Major
ST = I win

[And yet to times in hope my verse shall stand,
Praising thy worth, despite his cruel hand.] *End AF 3*

## Sonnet Eighty

### *AF 1*

PG/AC = I Open (I Honor)
QA = Star-Struckly
BP = The Pedestal (as if I put he or her on one)
OB = I want he or she to validate my love as he does my rival.
AM = Glad (Hope)
OS = Does he or she have anything to gain from my pleas?
CX = Major
ST = If he or she doesn't recognize my love, my own words (poetry)
    will be forever lost.

[O, how I faint when I of you do write,
Knowing a better spirit doth use your name,
And in the praise thereof spends all his might,
To make me tongue-tied, speaking of your fame!] *End AF 1*

### *AF 2*

PG/AC = I Close (I Accuse)
QA = Hurtfully
BP = The Competition (as in my competitor—he or she who my
    patron favors.)
OB = Same
AM = Mad
OS = Same
CX = Auxilliary
ST = Same

[But since your worth, wide as the ocean is,
The humble as the proudest sail doth bear,

My saucy bark inferior far to his
On your broad main doth wilfully appear.] *End AF 2*

### *AF 3*

PG/AC = I Throw (I Toss—away my pride.)
QA = Humbly
BP = The Bottom Line
OB = Same
AM = Glad
OS = Same
CX = Major
ST = Same

[Your shallowest help will hold me up afloat,
Whilst he upon your soundless deep doth ride;
Or being wreck'd, I am a worthless boat,
He of tall building and of goodly pride:
Then if he thrive and I be cast away,
The worst was this; my love was my decay.] *End AF 3*

**Note: The only reason to change PG's and QA is because you are not getting what you want in the manner in which you are pursuing the OB. Make sure you are taking the time to end one AF before moving onto another. There must be a transition between AF's.**

## Sonnet One Hundred-Sixteen

### *AF 1*

PG/AC = I Lift (I Unveil)
QA = Wholeheartedly
BP = The Absolute Truth
OB = I want he or she they? to admit that love is constant and
   unalterable.
AM = Glad
OS = He or she has a different opinion.
CX = Major
ST = Perhaps he or she is a rival and I must win my argument to
   be top dog.

# THE SONNETS

[Let me not to the marriage of true minds
Admit impediments. Love is not love
Which alters when it alteration finds,
Or bends with the remover to remove.
**(AX)** O no! it is an ever-fixed mark
That looks on tempests and is never shaken;
It is the star to every wandering bark,
Whose worth's unknown, although his height be taken.]
   *End AF 1*


## *AF 2*

PG/AC = I Embrace (I Share)
QA = Mockingly
BP = The Clarification
OB = Same
AM = Same
OS = Same
CX = Auxiliary
ST = Same

[Love's not Time's fool, though rosy lips and cheeks
Within his bending sickle's compass come:
Love alters not with his brief hours and weeks,
But bears it out even to the edge of doom.] *End AF 2*


## *AF 3*

PG/AC = I Smash (I Stand as in take a stand or stand firm.)
QA = By-Godly
BP = The Rock (unmovable and unshakeable)
OB = Same
AM = Same
OS = Same
CX = Major
ST = Same

[If this be error and upon me proved,
I never writ, nor no man ever loved.] *End AF 3*

# THE SONNETS

## Sonnet One Hundred-Thirty

### *AF 1*

PG/AC = I Embrace (I Possess)
QA = Lustfully
BP = The Exotic
OB = I want to exclaim my love.
AM = Glad
OS = Most people will not see the real beauty in my love.
CX = Major
ST = People have such a narrow view of beauty. It is a blight on our
  culture.


[My mistress' eyes are nothing like the sun;
Coral is far more red than her lips' red;
If snow be white, why then her breasts are dun;
If hairs be wires, black wires grow on her head.
I have seen roses damask'd, red and white,
But no such roses see I in her cheeks;
And in some perfumes is there more delight
Than in the breath that from my mistress reeks.] *End AF 1*


### *AF 2*

PG/AC = I Open (I Confess)
QA = Truthfully
BP = The Cards on the Table
OB = Same
AM = Same
OS = Same
CX = Auxiliary
ST = Same


[I love to hear her speak, yet well I know
That music hath a far more pleasing sound;
I grant I never saw a goddess go;
My mistress, when she walks, treads on the ground:] *End AF 2*

# THE SONNETS

29

### *AF 3*

PG/AC = I Push (I Press—my point.)
QA = Demonstratively
BP = The Heartstring
OB = Same
AM = Same
OS = Same
CX = Major
ST = Same

[And yet, by heaven, I think my love as rare
As any she belied with false compare.] *End AF 3*

## Sonnet One Hundred-Forty-Four

### *AF 1*

PG/AC = I Lift (I Weigh—the circumstances.)
QA = Admittedly
BP = The Premise
OB = I want to solve this problem.
AM = Fear (as in unknowing)
OS = Is there an answer—as I love them both?
CX = Auxiliary
ST = I may be in danger of losing one or the other or even each to
the other.

[Two loves I have of comfort and despair,
Which like two spirits do suggest me still:
The better angel is a man right fair,
The worser spirit a woman colour'd ill.] *End AF 1*

### *AF 2*

PG/AC = I Pull (I Debate)
QA = Scratch-headedly
BP = The Big Q

# THE SONNETS

OB = Same
AM = Same
OS = Same
CX = Major
ST = Same

[To win me soon to hell, my female evil
Tempteth my better angel from my side,
And would corrupt my saint to be a devil,
Wooing his purity with her foul pride.
And whether that my angel be turn'd fiend
Suspect I may, but not directly tell;
But being both from me, both to each friend,
I guess one angel in another's hell:] *End AF 2*


## *AF 3*

PG/AC = I Smash (I Give as in give-up.)
QA = Exasperatedly
BP = The Bitch (of it all)
OB = Same
AM = Mad
OS = Same
CX = Major
ST = Same

[Yet this shall I ne'er know, but live in doubt,
Till my bad angel fire my good one out.] *End AF 3*

**Notes: We have finished the section on sonnets and I'd like to offer
some tidbits concerning using the poems as audition pieces. I hope
the sonnets I chose to illustrate will give you a sense of the variety
inherent in them and the cornucopia of possibilities—especially those
possibilities in Action and Quality of Action not explored here.**

- **Avoid falling into the trap of playing the poetry. When you research
  the meaning of the sonnets you will find all sorts of scholarly com-
  ments which will not necessarily contribute to actually playing the**

THE SONNETS                                    31

material. Instead, strive to make the poetry active. Always have in your imagination the person to whom you are addressing. Play the Action (AC) and Quality of Action (QA) to reach your Objective (OB.) After all the AC and QA are the only two playable things in your toolbox. The rest is important certainly but not at all anything doable.

- Work on sonnets until you are comfortable with the template I have provided. The template is the actor's 'score.' Mastering 14 lines of iambic pentameter, including mastering your score, is of paramount importance prior to tackling the more difficult material that are monologues and soliloquies.
- It is very easy for the actor to skip over the endings of Artistic Frames (AF's). We all want to get to the climax. Yet, especially in Shakespeare, you have to earn the climax by paying equal attention to each and every moment. So, don't rush.
- Let's talk a bit more about creating a Rhythmical Wave (RW). There are certainly clues to creating an RW in the text and, hopefully, in the sample scores I have provided. Yet, it is the actor only who can produce the RW for audience to ride—and riding the wave is exactly the image we want to work with. We want the audience to be taken on a journey that is created by the RW. So, you must pay careful attention to tempo/rhythm, volume, operative words, punctuation, breath—where to breathe, vocal range, and, of course, scansion. Investing in all of this work is at first daunting. With the proper amount of work on the actor's part it will all become second nature.
- Please do not skip over the Atmosphere (AM) exercise in the Appendix. You don't need to do the exercise every time you stop and begin again. It should be done at the top of each individual rehearsal.
- As I have said, one of the Archetypes (AR) of the speaker in each sonnet is the Poet. Another AR inherent in the poems is that of the Lover. Look carefully at the definitions of these AR's and you'll find an 'in' to characterization. See the Appendix on how to use AR's in your work.

End Chapter Two

# Chapter Three

## THE COMEDIES – WOMEN

All monologues and soliloquies from the comedies are not necessarily funny even though they are from a comedic play. You'll also find comedic speeches in the tragedies. Sometimes it is the character who is humorous in the comedies rather than what the character is saying. I would point to Touchstone from *As You Like It* as an example in some of his speeches. Indeed, some other speeches are not comedic at all as in Titania's 'Forgeries of Jealously' speech from *Midsummer*. It really is all about the character within the given circumstances. In Shakespeare, you have a wealth of information to assist you in creating character. We will explore those elements in each speech via specific Archetypes. I say this because actors are often asked for contrasting monologues. This doesn't necessarily mean tragic and comic. It can easily be a contrast in character. Just don't choose two speeches from Medea or for that matter any other play. Light and semi-heavy is a good guide.

The Michael Chekhov Technique differs and soars above other methodologies when approaching character. You can practice the Imaginary Body exercise in Appendix I with each speech explored. Other techniques tend to focus on bringing 'self' to each role. Well, of course one must bring self to each role because YOU are playing it. There has always been the rule in Hollywood of casting the actor closest to the character in type. Once Hollywood producers see the actor is marketable they immediately find projects that actor can bring himself or herself to. There are some notable exceptions. Unfortunately, some/many LORT theaters across the country have adopted this kind of casting as well. It is past time for actors to take back the theater. After all, the actor is the most important player in the art form. We

# THE COMEDIES – WOMEN                    33

can begin by fighting type casting with our technique. The more characters we develop in our auditions the more casting directors will not see us as one type. The rule: know the character you are auditioning for and suit your material and character to that role. This means you must have a bag full of monologues ready—or at least ready to work on. You can approach this and truncate the process by looking for speeches with varying archetypes. Look at the archetype exercise in the Appendix.

In each speech I am going to only give the briefest of information concerning the given circumstances. I'll do this in a note at the end of each speech. There are excellent resources, including the play, to aid you in understanding the givens. The given circumstances of each play are not the focus of this book. In the monologues and soliloquies we will look mostly at the same things we explored in the sonnets with added suggestions of archetypes.

An archetype is not something one can play. It is simply a part of the given circumstances the playwright gives you. You create the archetype via Imaginary Body and adopting mannerisms—which Chekhov calls 'Jewelry.' Physicalize the archetype and then begin creating your score. You may think there are more archetypes listed than necessary. Major characters in Shakespeare indeed possess more archetypes than in contemporary work. It's because the scope of his plays is broader and his characters muse on very big ideas. Regardless, the archetypes listed are meant for the entire play and for individual speeches as indicated.

Finally, I don't make much mention of Rhythmical Wave (RW) in the scores. If you follow the template provided the RW will take care of itself.

**Note: I have made cuts in some speeches.**

**Note: All AF's are bracketed [].**

## One

*As You Like It*
Act III, sc. iv

Phoebe—AR's—Abandoned/Orphan Child, Seductress, Damsel, Lover

# MONOLOGUE

**Note: Use the first QA listed in the score continually until there is a change indicated.**

## *AF 1*

PG/AC = I Push/I Reject
QA = Defiantly
BP = The Declaration
OB = I want Ganymede to love me back!
AM = Mad
OS = Ganymede showed no signs of attraction to me.
CX = Major
ST = I have met the love of my life. I can't lose him.

**AR (Lover)** [Think not I love him, though I ask for him.] *End AF 1*

## *AF 2*

PG/AC = I Wring/I Compare
QA = Derogatorily
BP = The Judgement
OB = Same
AM = Fear (as in not knowing-contemplating)
OS = same
CX = Auxiliary
ST = Same

'Tis but a peevish boy; **QA (Admiringly)** yet he talks well;
**QA (Not need-ed-ly)** But what care I for words? **QA (Truthfully)** Yet words do well
When he that speaks them pleases those that hear.
**QA (Wantonly) (AX)** It is a pretty youth: **QA (Backing-off-a-bitly)** not very pretty;

**Note: Remember AX is a spike in AT. When you encounter an AX in the text it does not necessarily mean louder. Rather, it is an investment**

# THE COMEDIES – WOMEN

from the actor to heighten her or his subjective atmosphere. It is an inward commitment to the given circumstances. In our Technique it is an Expansion. Please see Appendix I for an explanation and exercise of Expansion–Contraction.

> **QA (Judgingly)** But, sure, he's proud, **QA (On-the-other-handly)** and yet his pride becomes him;

**Note: Anytime you feel you are not quite matching your vocal quality with the QA simply speak the QA with the line. . . 'On the other handly . . . his pride becomes him:' For rehearsal purposes only of course.**

> **QA (Absolutely)** He'll make a proper man: **QA (Excitedly)** the best thing in him
> Is his complexion; and faster than his tongue
> Did make offence his eye did heal it up.
> **QA (Regretfully)** He is not very tall; **QA (Happily)** yet for his years he's tall.
> **QA (Unfortunately)** His leg is but so so; **QA (But what-of-it-ly)** and yet 'tis well.] *End AF 2*

### *AF 3*

PG/AC = I Smash (I Squash—the notion)
QA = Sarcastically
BP = The Cover (my ass)
OB = Same
AM = Mad (on the milder side)
OS = Same
CX = Auxiliary
ST = Same

[There be some women, Silvius, had they mark'd him
In parcels as I did, would have gone near
To fall in love with him, but, for my part,
I love him not nor hate him not; and yet
I have more cause to hate him than to love him.] *End AF 3*

# THE COMEDIES – WOMEN

## AF 4

PG/AC = I Penetrate (I Press—the matter)
QA = Begrudgingly
BP = The Realization
OB = Same
AM = Mad (more than last AF)
OS = Same
CX = Major
ST = Same

[For what had he to do to chide at me?
He said mine eyes were black and my hair black:
And, now I am remember'd, scorn'd at me:
**QA (Full-of-myself-ed-ly)** I marvel why I answer'd not again.] *End
AF 4*

## AF 5

PG/AC = I Embrace (I Seduce)
QA = Cunningly
BP = The Plan
OB = Same
AM = Glad
OS = Same
CX = Major
ST = Same

[But that's all one; omittance is no quittance.
I'll write to him a very taunting letter,
And thou shalt bear it: **QA (Seductively)** wilt thou, Silvius?] *End
AF 5*

**Note: Phoebe is speaking to Silvius. He is in absolute love/lust with her. In this speech she plays him like a fine fiddle to get him to do her bidding. It is interesting that Phoebe is basically espousing her own love/lust for Ganymede in front of the person she knows loves her. She knows all the right buttons to push. Invest in her archetypes and work diligently on all of the QA changes. It might also be prudent to**

# THE COMEDIES – WOMEN

37

work on the **Imaginary Body of Seductress** for this speech. Phoebe turns that archetype on and off easily.

It is the wonderful quick changes in QA that create the RW in this piece. Be careful with the changes. It is easy to fall into two energies when weighing the issues Phoebe weighs. In other words, each QA has its own energy in tempo/rhythm, volume, etc. The more varied the QA's the better.

## Two

*As You Like It*
Act III, sc. v

Rosalind—AR's—Abandoned/Orphan Child, Lover, Companion, Gambler, Liberator, Princess, Rebel, Savior

## MONOLOGUE

**Note: The larger the role the more AR's you'll find. The AR's arise depending on the given circumstances. Here you'll find nuances in Imaginary Body and Jewelry.**

### *AF 1*

PG/AC = I Push (I Challenge)
QA = Angrily
BP = The Place (as in put her in her place)
OB = I want to come to the rescue of Silvius.
AM = Mad
OS = If she sees through my disguise I'm sunk.
CX = Major
ST = Having been there, I have to right some wrongs in the world. It is my destiny.

**AR (Liberator)** [And why, I pray you? Who might be your mother, That you insult, exult, and all at once, Over the wretched? **QA (Insultingly)** What though you have no beauty—
As, by my faith, I see no more in you

Than without candle may go dark to bed—
Must you be therefore proud and pitiless?] *End AF 1*

### *AF 2*

PG/AC = I Open (I Exclaim)
QA = Unbelievably
BP = The Realization
OB = Same
AM = Bad
OS = Same
CX = Auxiliary
ST = Same

**AR (Princess)** [Why, what means this? Why do you look on me?
I see no more in you than in the ordinary
Of nature's sale-work. 'Od's my little life,
I think she means to tangle my eyes too!
No, faith, proud mistress, hope not after it:
**QA (Disgustingly)** 'Tis not your inky brows, your black silk hair,
Your bugle eyeballs, nor your cheek of cream,
That can entame my spirits to your worship.] *End AF 2*

### *AF 3*

PG/AC = I Lift (I Bolster)
QA = Emboldenly
BP = The Booster
OB = Same
AM = Glad
OS = Same
CX = Auxiliary
ST = Same

**AR (Liberator)** [You foolish shepherd, wherefore do you follow
     her,
Like foggy south puffing with wind and rain?
You are a thousand times a properer man

# THE COMEDIES – WOMEN

Than she a woman: 'tis such fools as you
That makes the world full of ill-favour'd children.
**QA (Brotherly)** 'Tis not her glass, but you, that flatters her;
And out of you she sees herself more proper
Than any of her lineaments can show her.] *End AF 3*

## *AF 4*

PG/AC = I Smash  (I Demand)
QA = Ruthlessy
BP = The Brand (as if Phoebe has been branded)
OB = Same
AM = Glad
OS = Same
CX = Major
ST = Same

**AR (Rebel)** [But, mistress, know yourself: down on your knees,
And thank heaven, fasting, for a good man's love;
For I must tell you friendly in your ear,
**QA (Cuttingly)** Sell when you can: you are not for all markets.] *End AF 4*

## *AF 5*

PG/AC = I Close  (I Seal—the deal)
QA = Forcefully
BP = The Closing Argument
OB = Same
AM = Sad
OS = Same
CX = Major
ST = Same

**AR (Savior)** [Cry the man mercy; love him; take his offer;
Foul is most foul, being foul to be a scoffer.
**QA (Paternally)** So take her to thee, shepherd: fare you well.] *End AF 5*

40     THE COMEDIES – WOMEN

**Note: Rosalind (Ganymede) is one of Shakespeare's 'pants' roles. In this speech Rosalind is dressed in men's clothes and is mistaken for a man by Phoebe and Silvius. This speech, in the play, takes place just prior to the previous speech of Phoebe's we first looked at.**

**Embrace the archetypes in this monologue. Remember there is an archetype exercise in the Appendix.**

# Three

*The Comedy of Errors*
Act III, sc. ii

Luciana—AR's—Dependent Child, Princess, Lover, Samaritan

## MONOLOGUE

### *AF 1*

PG/AC = I Push/I Accuse
QA = Hotly
BP = The Accusation
OB = I want him to treat my sister with due respect.
AM = Mad
OS = I am talking to a man in man's world.
CX = Major
ST = I and the entire family may suffer social admonishment. Ruin!

**AR (Princess)** [And may it be that you have quite forgot
A husband's office? Shall, Antipholus,
Even in the spring of love, thy love-springs rot?
Shall love, in building, grow so ruinous?] *End AF 1*

### *AF 2*

PG/AC = I Pull/I Reason
QA = Calmly
BP = The Making Sense
OB = Same
AM = Fear

OS = Same
CX = Auxiliary
ST = Same

**AR (Samaritan)** [If you did wed my sister for her wealth,
Then for her wealth's sake use her with more kindness;
Or if you like elsewhere, do it by stealth.
Muffle your false love with some show of blindness:
Let not my sister read it in your eye;
Be not thy tongue thy own shame's orator.
**QA (Sweetly)** Look sweet, be fair, become disloyalty;
Apparel vice like virtue's harbinger;
Bear a fair presence, though your heart be tainted;
Teach sin the carriage of a holy saint;
Be secret-false: what need she be acquainted?] *End AF 2*


### *AF 3*

PG/AC = I Wring/I Chide
QA = Lovingly sarcastic
BP = The Big Squeeze
OB = Same
AM = Mad
OS = Same
CX = Auxiliary
ST = Same

**AR (Princess)** [What simple thief brags of his own attaint?
'Tis double wrong, to truant with your bed
And let her read it in thy looks at board.
Shame hath a bastard fame, well managed;
Ill deeds are doubled with an evil word.] *End AF 3*


### *AF 4*

PG/AC = I Open/I Beg
QA = Pleadingly
BP = The Meltdown

42            THE COMEDIES – WOMEN

OB = Same
AM = Fear
OS = Same
CX = Major
ST = Same

**AR (Dependent Child)** [Alas, poor women!—Make us but believe,
Being compact of credit, that you love us;
Though others have the arm, show us the sleeve;
We in your motion turn and you may move us.] *End AF 4*

## *AF 5*

PG/AC = I Close/I Conclude
QA = Weepily
BP = The Final Round
OB = Same
AM = Sad
OS = Same
CX = Auxiliary
ST = Same

**AR (Samaritan)** [Then, gentle brother, get you in again;
Comfort my sister, cheer her, call her wife:
'Tis holy sport to be a little vain,
When the sweet breath of flattery conquers strife.] *End AF 5*

**Note: Luciana does not know she is talking to her sister's twin brother
who has never met Luciana and has no idea of what she is talking about.
He is new to the town—he doesn't know his brother resides there nor
does he know his brother's wife. Luciana's sister is distraught, thinking
after meeting with the twin brother, that her husband doesn't love her
anymore. The twin Antipholus has absolutely denied even knowing
Adriana—Luciana's sister.**

**Be careful with the rhyming couplets. Use your operative words and
you won't fall into a pattern of stressing all equally. Be sure to give
varied weight to operative words.**

# THE COMEDIES – WOMEN

43

## Four

*The Merchant of Venice*
Act III, sc. iv

Portia—AR's—Eternal Child, Princess, Samaritan, Politician, Rescuer, Feminist, Lawyer

## MONOLOGUE

### *AF 1*

PG/AC = I Strike/I Claim
QA = Anticipatedly (constantly changing)
BP = The Proving Ground
OB = I want to prove my worth.
AM = Glad
OS = Keeping her plan quiet. No one, other than Nerissa, can know.
CX = Major (building)
ST = Losing my worth in society!

**AR (Princess)** [Come on, Nerissa; I have work in hand
That you yet know not of: we'll see our husbands
Before they think of us—
**QA (Consideringly)**—but in such a habit,
That they shall think we are accomplished
With that we lack. **QA (Cocklily)** I'll hold thee any wager,
When we are both accoutred like young men,
I'll prove the prettier fellow of the two,
And wear my dagger with the braver grace,
And speak between the change of man and boy
With a reed voice, and turn two mincing steps
Into a manly stride, and speak of frays
Like a fine bragging youth, and tell quaint lies,
How honourable ladies sought my love,
Which I denying, they fell sick and died;
I could not do withal.] *End AF 1*

# THE COMEDIES – WOMEN

## *AF 2*

PG/AC = I Close/I Conceal
QA = Weepily
BP = The Ruse
OB = Same
AM = Sad
OS = Same
CX = Auxiliary
ST = Same

**AR—Politician** [Then I'll repent,
And wish for all that, that I had not killed them;
And twenty of these puny lies I'll tell,
That men shall swear I have discontinued school
Above a twelvemonth. **QA (Cunningly)** I have within my mind
A thousand raw tricks of these bragging Jacks,
Which I will practise.] *End AF 2*

## *AF 3*

PG/AC = I Open/I Order
QA = Hurriedly
BP = The Plan
OB = Same
AM = Glad
OS = Same
CX = Auxiliary
ST = Same

**AR (Rescuer)** [But come, I'll tell thee all my whole device
When I am in my coach, which stays for us
At the park gate; and therefore haste away,
For we must measure twenty miles to-day.] *End AF 3*

**Note: This is a wonderful speech that is not particularly overdone because it requires tremendous breath control and careful building. Portia is elated to have an opportunity to accomplish a brave deed in a man's world. It will require courage and cunning.**

# THE COMEDIES – WOMEN 45

Work hard on the changes of QA. They should be like 'spring-boards.' Each new quality should spring into a new thought with increased energy.

You will have noticed that QA's can constantly change. That doesn't necessarily mean that your AC or OB needs to change. In fact, it is much simpler and more dynamic for the actor to look for QA changes in AF's. QA's are the territory of the actor and the actor only!

## Five

*The Merchant of Venice*
Act IV, sc. i

Portia—AR's—Eternal Child, Princess, Samaritan, Politician, Rescuer, Feminist, Lawyer

## MONOLOGUE

### *AF 1*

PG/AC = I Penetrate/I Reason
QA = Restrainedly or Reservedly
BP = The Plea
OB = I want to save Antonio's life!
AM = Fear
OS = Shylock's reluctance to reason
CX = Major (building)
ST = Antonio will die if judgement goes Shylock's way.

**AR (Lawyer)** [The quality of mercy is not strain'd,
It droppeth as the gentle rain from heaven

**Note: Shakespeare often gives you the QA in the text. Restrainedly comes from 'gentle rain.' Be aware of other QA clues.**

Upon the place beneath: **QA (Reverently)** It is twice blest;
It blesseth him that gives and him that takes.
**QA (Majestically)** 'Tis mightiest in the mightiest: it becomes
The throned monarch better than his crown;

**Note: Be careful to build slowly. Don't blow it all from the beginning of the AF.**

# THE COMEDIES – WOMEN

His sceptre shows the force of temporal power,
The attribute to awe and majesty,
Wherein doth sit the dread and fear of kings;
But mercy is above this sceptred sway:
It is enthroned in the hearts of kings,
It is an attribute to God himself;
And earthly power doth then show likest God's
When mercy seasons justice.] *End AF 1* **Line continued in next AF**

## *AF 2*

PG/AC = I Push/I Test—the boundaries
QA = Dangerously
BP = The Insult
OB = Same
AM = Mad
OS = Same
CX = Auxiliary
ST = Same

[Therefore, Jew,
Though justice be thy plea, consider this:] *End AF 2*

## *AF 3*

PG/AC = I Lift (I Unveil—the truth)
QA = Professorily
BP = The Whole Enchilada
OB = Same
AM = Glad
OS = Same
CX = Major
ST = Same

That, in the course of justice, none of us
Should see salvation. We do pray for mercy;
And that same prayer doth teach us all to render
The deeds of mercy.] *End AF 3* **Line continued in next AF**

# THE COMEDIES – WOMEN    47

## *AF 4*

PG/AC = I Close/I Close—the argument
QA = Factually
BP = The Closing
OB = Same
AM = Mad
OS = Same
CX = Auxiliary
ST = Same

[I have spoke thus much
To mitigate the justice of thy plea;
Which if thou follow, this strict court of Venice
Must needs give sentence 'gainst the merchant there.] *End AF 4*

**Note: Portia is disguised as a male. She has 'papers' from a well-known lawyer introducing her to the court in Venice.**

**We often see this speech done heatedly throughout—a trap. Take your time with this one. Don't fall into another trap that is every word has been thought out beforehand. Portia has thought about what she will say, yet she must and does react to Shylock's arguments spontaneously. This will keep the speech alive for you.**

## Six

*A Midsummer Night's Dream*
Act I, sc. i

Helena—AR's—Wounded Child, Princess, Addict, Lover, Deva, Dreamer, Rebel, Muse

## MONOLOGUE

## *AF 1*

PG/AC = I Close (I Retreat)
QA = Self-deprecatingly
BP = The Sorrow (as if in feeling sorry for myself)

OB = I want to find a way to win my love!
AM = Sad
OS = Hermia has the love of Demetrius.
CX = Major
ST = I will die unless I can have Demetrius

**AR (Wounded Child)** [Call you me fair? that fair again unsay.
Demetrius loves your fair: O happy fair!
Your eyes are lode-stars; and your tongue's sweet air
More tuneable than lark to shepherd's ear,
When wheat is green, when hawthorn buds appear.] *End AF 1*

PG/AC = I Open/I Admire
QA = Complimentary
BP = The Friendship
OB = Same
AM = Sad
OS = Same
CX = Auxiliary
ST = Same

[Sickness is catching: O, were favour so,
Yours would I catch, fair Hermia, ere I go;
My ear should catch your voice, my eye your eye,
My tongue should catch your tongue's sweet melody.
Were the world mine, Demetrius being bated,
The rest I'd give to be to you translated.] *End AF 2*

### *AF 3*

PG/AC = I Embrace/I Beg
QA = Sincerely
BP = The Plea
OB = Same
AM = Fear
OS = Same
CX = Major
ST = Same

# THE COMEDIES – WOMEN 49

[O, teach me how you look, and with what art
You sway the motion of Demetrius' heart.] *End AF 3*

**Note: Helena is talking to her best friend, Hermia. Demetrius has forsaken Helena for his love of Hermia. Hermia is in love with Lysander and not interested in Demetrius. So, Helena is both jealous of Hermia and needs her help to win Demetrius back.**

**The trap of this speech is to self-deprecate throughout or to be over-friendly throughout. Surely, Helena is experiencing more than just one emotion battling with this problem.**

## Seven

*A Midsummer Night's Dream*
Act I, sc. i

Helena—AR's—Wounded Child, Princess, Addict, Lover, Deva, Dreamer, Rebel, Muse

**Note: As this is the first soliloquy, I should reveal a strong belief I have about playing it and all other soliloquies. Obviously, there is no one on stage to play to. So, who is the character talking to and what could possibly be her objective? It is the audience. In most soliloquies the character is trying to solve a problem. In this speech Helena is musing on love and attempting to figure a way to win Demetrius. It is very active to use the audience as a literal scene partner. Rally the audience to your aid! Convince them to be on your side on your journey. What a journey it is. Invest in all of the wonderful QA changes and you'll have a blast—so will the audience.**

### *AF 1*

PG/AC = I Strike/Proclaim
QA = By-God-ed-ly
BP = The Truth
OB = I want to find a way to win my love!
AM = Mad
OS = Hermia has the love of Demetrius.

50    THE COMEDIES – WOMEN

CX = Major
ST = I will die unless I can have Demetrius!

**AR (Wounded Child)** [How happy some o'er other some can be!
Through Athens I am thought as fair as she.] *End AF 1*

*AF 2*

PG/AC = I Close/I Reject
QA = Sorrowfully
BP = The Reality Check
OB = Same
AM = Sad
OS = Same
CX = Auxiliary (building)
ST = Same

[But what of that? Demetrius thinks not so;
He will not know what all but he do know:
And as he errs, doting on Hermia's eyes,
So I, admiring of his qualities.
**QA (Realizingly)** Things base and vile, folding no quantity,
Love can transpose to form and dignity:
**QA (Contemplatively)** Love looks not with the eyes, but with the mind;
**QA (Realizingly 2)** And therefore is wing'd Cupid painted blind:
Nor hath Love's mind of any judgement taste;
Wings and no eyes figure unheedy haste.
**QA (Yepily)** And therefore is Love said to be a child,

**\*Note: Say the word 'Yep,' before 'therefore' and instead of 'And.'
You'll hear what it means.**

Because in choice he is so oft beguiled.
As waggish boys in game themselves forswear,
So the boy Love is perjured everywhere:
**QA (Factually)** For ere Demetrius look'd on Hermia's eyne,
He hail'd down oaths that he was only mine;
And when this hail some heat from Hermia felt,
So he dissolved, and showers of oaths did melt.] *End AF 2*

## THE COMEDIES – WOMEN                    51

### *AF 3*

PG/AC = I Embrace/I Seal-the plan
QA = Determinedly
BP = The Solution
OB = Same
AM = Glad
OS = Same
CX = Major
ST = Same

[I will go tell him of fair Hermia's flight:
Then to the wood will he to-morrow night
Pursue her; and for this intelligence
If I have thanks, it is a dear expense:
But herein mean I to enrich my pain,
To have his sight thither and back again.] *End AF 3*

**Note: By 'Realizingly' and 'Realizingly 2,' I mean that the second
realization should be more energetic. Things are occurring to Helena
in this speech for the first time and she is getting excited about the
process. By the end she should be in a frenzy. She might even thank the
audience for helping her.**

### Eight

*A Midsummer Night's Dream*
Act II, sc. i

Titania—AR's—Magical Child, Nature Child, Queen, Lover,
Dreamer, Mother/Matriarch, Teacher

### MONOLOGUE

### *AF 1*

PG/AC = I Strike (I Accuse)
QA = Accusatorially
BP = The Naked Truth
OB = I want Oberon to change his Actions towards humans.

# 52

## THE COMEDIES – WOMEN

AM = Mad
OS = Oberon never gives anything for nothing. He is stubborn.
CX = Major
ST = Humankind is suffering greatly.

**AR (Matriarch)** [These are the forgeries of jealousy:
And never, since the middle summer's spring,
Met we on hill, in dale, forest or mead,
By paved fountain or by rushy brook,
Or in the beached margent of the sea,
To dance our ringlets to the whistling wind,
But with thy brawls thou hast disturb'd our sport.] *End AF 1*

### *AF 2*

PG/AC = I Pull/I Inform
QA = Pitifully
BP = The Plague
OB = Same
AM = Sad
OS = Same
CX = Auxiliary
ST = Same

**AR (Nature Child)** [Therefore the winds, piping to us in vain,
As in revenge, have suck'd up from the sea
Contagious fogs; which falling in the land
Have every pelting river made so proud
That they have overborne their continents.
The ox hath therefore stretch'd his yoke in vain,
The ploughman lost his sweat, and the green corn
Hath rotted ere his youth attain'd a beard.] *End AF 2*

### *AF 3*

PG/AC = I Lift/I Teach
QA = Reasonably
BP = The Last Stand

THE COMEDIES – WOMEN      53

OB = Same
AM = Fear (veiled)

**Note: In the Chekhov Technique 'veiled' means to attempt to hide your true feelings.**

OS = Same
CX = Major
ST = Same

**AR (Teacher)** [The human mortals want their winter here;
No night is now with hymn or carol blest.
Therefore the moon, the governess of floods,
Pale in her anger, washes all the air,
That rheumatic diseases do abound:
**(AX)** And thorough this distemperature we see
The seasons alter, the spring, the summer,
The childing autumn, angry winter, change
Their wonted liveries, and the mazed world,
By their increase, now knows not which is which,
**(AX)** And this same progeny of evils comes
From our debate, from our dissension:
**QA (Definitively)** We are their parents and original.] *End AF 3*

**Note: Titania must take care with Oberon for she knows his temper. So, be careful in building this speech. You cannot afford to 'lose your cool' and risk your objective. Sure, Titania is seething inside—yet she absolutely must maintain her calm. Build the speech toward losing your temper but never get there—check yourself and begin again.**

**Polarity (PL) is achieved by change in QA's and in the manner in which you build each speech.**

## Nine

*Twelfth Night*
Act II, sc. ii

Viola—AR's—Devine Child, Diplomat, Networker, Pilgrim, Samaritan, Lover

# SOLILOQUY

## *AF 1*

PG/AC = I Throw/I Ponder
QA = Quizzically
BP = The Realization
OB = I want to solve this problem.
AM = Fear
OS = I am disguised as a man.
CX = Auxiliary with a Major AX
ST = Unless I sort this out I will not be able to win the person I'm
   in love with!


**AR (Lover)** [I left no ring with her: what means this lady?
**(AX)** Fortune forbid my outside have not charm'd her!
She made good view of me; indeed, so much,
That sure methought her eyes had lost her tongue,
For she did speak in starts distractedly.
**QA (Oh-my-God-ed-ly)** She loves me, sure; the cunning of her passion
Invites me in this churlish messenger.
**QA (Factually)** None of my lord's ring. Why, he sent her none;
I am the man. **QA (Sorrowfully)** If it be so, as 'tis,
Poor lady, she were better love a dream.
**QA (Angrily)** Disguise, I see, thou art a wickedness,
Wherein the pregnant enemy does much.
**(AX)** How easy is it for the proper-false
In women's waxen hearts to set their forms.
Alas, our frailty is the cause, not we!
For such as we are made of, such we be.] *End AF 1*


## *AF 2*

PG/AC = I Open
QA = Puzzlingly
BP = The Review
OB = Same
AM = Same

# THE COMEDIES – WOMEN

55

OS = Same
CX = Major
ST = Same

[How will this fadge? My master loves her dearly;
And I, poor monster, fond as much on him;
And she, mistaken, seems to dote on me.
What will become of this? **QA (Conflictedly)** As I am man,
My state is desperate for my master's love,
As I am woman—now alas the day!—
What thriftless sighs shall poor Olivia breathe!
**QA (Pleadingly) (AX)** O time, thou must untangle this, not I,
It is too hard a knot for me to untie!] *End AF 2*

**Note: When you encounter an AX in the text it does not necessarily mean louder. Rather, it is an investment from the actor to heighten her or his subjective atmosphere. It is an inward commitment to the given circumstances. In our Technique it is an Expansion.**

## Ten

*Twelfth Night*
Act III, sc. i

Olivia—AR's—Child Eternal, Lover, Princess, Victim

## MONOLOGUE

### *AF 1*

PG/AC = I Close/I Remind
QA = Earnestly
BP = The Reminder
OB = I want to move onto the more important subject.
AM = Fear
OS = Cesario may be offended.
CX = Auxiliary
ST = I could possibly lose him before I show my hand.

**AR (Victim)** [O, by your leave, I pray you,
I bade you never speak again of him.] *End AF 1*

### AF 2

PG/AC = I Open (I Profess)
QA = Lovingly
BP = The Confession
OB = To win my love to my heart!
AM = Fear
OS = Cesario
CX = Major
ST = Not knowing his heart my love for Cesario might not be
    returned.

**AR (Lover)** [But, would you undertake another suit,
I had rather hear you to solicit that
Than music from the spheres.

**(Cut Line) VIOLA**
Dear lady,—

**OLIVIA**
**QA (Beggingly)** Give me leave, beseech you. **QA (Nervously)** I did
    send,
After the last enchantment you did here,
A ring in chase of you: so did I abuse
Myself, my servant and, I fear me, you.
**(AX)** Under your hard construction must I sit,
To force that on you, in a shameful cunning,
Which you knew none of yours: what might you think?
**(AX)** Have you not set mine honour at the stake
And baited it with all the unmuzzled thoughts
That tyrannous heart can think? To one of your receiving
Enough is shown: a cypress, not a bosom,
Hideth my heart. **PG (I Embrace/I Grasp)** So, let me hear you
    speak.] *End AF 2*

# THE COMEDIES – WOMEN

57

**Note: PG** changes are completely subjective as is all of the work in these scores. The score appears from the way I have acted them and then conducted painstaking spy-back on my work. In the end the work will be yours, and you can change AC, QA, and PG's as you discover your own journey in the speeches. There is something I would caution you on: don't overburden the text with change for change sake.

## Eleven

*The Two Gentlemen of Verona*
Act I, sc. ii

Julia—AR—Eternal Child, Princess, Lover, Victim

**Note: There** are times when one might make a case that a single, even long, speech may have only one AF and alter PG's without changing the objective. This speech meets the criteria. Note the many QA and PG changes that help create the RW that we strive for.

Julia has just torn to pieces a letter from Proteus, one of her many suitors. She wishes she hadn't.

## SOLILOQUY

### *AF 1*

PG/AC = I Tear/I Tear (at my heart strings)
QA = Regretfully
BP = The Mess (I've made)
OB = I want to find out the content of the letter.
AM = Mad
OS = I've torn the letter to pieces.
CX = Major
ST = I prefer Proteus above any suitor and I may have destroyed a
    letter filled with his proclaiming his love for me!

**AR (Lover)** [O hateful hands, to tear such loving words!
Injurious wasps, to feed on such sweet honey
And kill the bees that yield it with your stings!

# 58 THE COMEDIES – WOMEN

**QA (Sweetly)** I'll kiss each several paper for amends.
Look, here is writ 'kind Julia.' **QA (Angrily) (AX)** Unkind Julia!
As in revenge of thy ingratitude,
I throw thy name against the bruising stones,
Trampling contemptuously on thy disdain.
**QA (Mournfully)** And here is writ 'love-wounded Proteus.'
Poor wounded name! My bosom as a bed
Shall lodge thee till thy wound be thoroughly heal'd;
And thus I search it with a sovereign kiss.
**QA (Wonderingly)** But twice or thrice was 'Proteus' written
down.
Be calm, good wind, blow not a word away
Till I have found each letter in the letter,
Except mine own name: that some whirlwind bear
Unto a ragged fearful-hanging rock
And throw it thence into the raging sea!
**QA (Passionately)** Lo, here in one line is his name twice writ,
'Poor forlorn Proteus, passionate Proteus,
To the sweet Julia:' **QA (Angrily) (AX)** that I'll tear away.
**QA (Lovingly)** And yet I will not, sith so prettily
He couples it to his complaining names.
**QA (Dutifully)** Thus will I fold them one on another:
**PG (I Embrace/I Enfold) QA (Made-Up-My-Mindedly)** Now kiss,
embrace, contend, do what you will.] *End AF 1*

**Note: Build the speech according to the AX's and QA's. It's easy with
this one to fall into a trap of raging throughout. The QA's will save you
from that trap. I could also challenge you to find more PG's. Yet, don't
overcomplicate.**

## Twelve

**Note: Julia is contemplating a portrait of Silvia. Proteus, the
would-be love of Julia, has now turned his affections toward Silvia.**

*The Two Gentlemen of Verona*
Act IV, sc. iv

Julia—AR—Eternal Child, Princess, Lover, Victim

# THE COMEDIES – WOMEN

## SOLILOQUY

### *AF 1*

PG/AC = I Open/I Realize
QA = Shockingly
BP = The Jealous Me
OB = I want Proteus for my own!
AM = Fear
OS = Proteus now favors Silvia.
CX = Major
ST = I may not win the person I love with Silvia in the way!

**AR (Lover)** [A virtuous gentlewoman, mild and beautiful!] *End AF 1*

### *AF 2*

PG/AC = I Open/I Reason

**\*Note: You can always reinvest in a PG where appropriate. It is akin to an AX.**

QA = Hopefully
BP = The Contemplation
OB = Same
AM = Same
OS = Same
CX = Auxiliary
ST = Same

**AR (Victim)** [I hope my master's suit will be but cold,
Since she respects my mistress' love so much.
Alas, how love can trifle with itself!] *End AF 2*

### *AF 3*

PG/AC = I Close/I Study
QA = Comparatively
BP = The Sizing Up
OB = Same
AM = Same

# 60      THE COMEDIES – WOMEN

OS = Same

CX = Auxiliary (with a careful build)

ST = Same

**AR (Lover)** [Here is her picture: let me see; I think,

If I had such a tire, this face of mine

Were full as lovely as is this of hers;

**QA (Derogatorily)** And yet the painter flatter'd her a little,

**QA (Comparatively)** Unless I flatter with myself too much.

**QA (Every-day-ly)** Her hair is auburn, **PG (I Open/I Brag) QA (Glowingly)** mine is perfect

yellow:

**QA (Solvingly)** If that be all the difference in his love,

I'll get me such a colour'd periwig.

**PG (I Close/I Close) QA (It's a drawly)** Her eyes are grey as glass, and so are mine:

**PG (I Open/I Open) QA (Happily)** Ay, but her forehead's low, and mine's as high.

**PG (I Close/I Open) QA (Angrily)** What should it be that he respects in her

**Note: We don't always need to state an AC other than the PG. In fact, the more you use this Technique the less you'll need to specify the AC beyond the PG.**

But I can make respective in myself,

If this fond Love were not a blinded god?] *End AF 3*

## *AF 4*

**PG/AC = I Pull/I Command (myself)**

QA = Determinedly

BP = The Path

OB = Same

AM = Mad

OS = Same

CX = Major

ST = Same

**(AX)** Come, shadow, come and take this shadow up,

For 'tis thy rival. **PG (I Tear/I Pledge)** O thou senseless form,

THE COMEDIES – WOMEN 61

Thou shalt be worshipp'd, kiss'd, loved and adored!
And, were there sense in his idolatry,
My substance should be statue in thy stead.
**QA (Kindly)** I'll use thee kindly for thy mistress' sake,
That used me so; **QA (Heatedly) (AX)** or else, by Jove I vow,
I should have scratch'd out your unseeing eyes
To make my master out of love with thee!] *End AF 4*

## APPLICATION OF THE MICHAEL CHEKHOV TECHNIQUE TO SHAKESPEARE'S MONOLOGUES AND SOLILOQUIES

### *THE COMEDIES-MEN*

### One

*As You Like It*
Act II, sc. i

**Note: There are two Dukes in this play. Duke Senior has a younger brother who has usurped the elder's dukedom. The role is most often played by the same actor. It sets up a perfect archetypal opposite. Duke Senior represents the good character—his brother—evil. Duke Senior is a loving lord and is a sympathetic and simple character. He is speaking to the followers who fled to the Forest of Arden with him. Hint: You can plan the reactions of the gang following each question. Also, it's really cold.**

Duke Senior—AR—Eternal Child, Prince, Lover, Victim, Rescuer, Father

### MONOLOGUE

### *AF 1*

PG/AC = I Lift/I Motivate
QA = Enthusiastically
BP = The Pre-Game Speech
OB = I want my comrades to embrace our situation and make the best of it.

62 THE COMEDIES – WOMEN

AM = Fear (Remember the folks are cold, hungry, and miss the creature comforts. Duke Senior is combating the objective atmosphere of Fear with his subjective atmosphere.)
OS = Explained in AM
CX = Major
ST = The men (and women) with me may give up and return to court. I may never get my lands and family back.

**AR (Rescuer)** [Now, my co-mates and brothers in exile,
Hath not old custom made this life more sweet
Than that of painted pomp? **QA (Leadingly)** Are not these woods
More free from peril than the envious court?
**QA (Preachily)** Here feel we but the penalty of Adam,
The seasons' difference, as the icy fang
And churlish chiding of the winter's wind,
Which, when it bites and blows upon my body,
Even till I shrink with cold, **QA (Lovingly)** I smile and say
'This is no flattery: **QA (Factually)** these are counsellors
That feelingly persuade me what I am.'] *End AF 1*


## *AF 2*

PG/AC = I Lift/I Motivate (a reinvestment, so, an AX)
QA = Desperately
BP = The Half-Time Speech
OB = Same
AM = Same
OS = Same
CX = Major
ST = Same

[**(AX)** Sweet are the uses of adversity,
**QA (Disgustingly)** Which, like the toad, ugly and venomous,
Wears yet a precious jewel in his head;
**QA (Poetically)** And this our life exempt from public haunt
Finds tongues in trees, books in the running brooks,
Sermons in stones and good in everything.
**QA (Weepily)** I would not change it.] *End AF 2*

# THE COMEDIES – WOMEN 63

## Two

*As You Like It*
Act II, sc. i

First Lord—AR—Orphan Child, Poet, Lover, Victim

## MONOLOGUE

### *AF 1*

PG/AC = I Open/I Reveal
QA = Bluntly
BP = The Cards on the Table
OB = I want the Duke to see both sides of the debate. (**See note at bottom.**)
AM = Fear (of reprisal)
OS = The Duke may not be open to hearing the truth.
CX = Auxiliary
ST = I may be banished from the forest for my statements.

**AR (Victim)** [Indeed, my lord,
The melancholy Jaques grieves at that,
And, in that kind, swears you do more usurp
Than doth your brother that hath banish'd you.] *End AF 1*

### *AF 2*

PG/AC = I Pull/I Reel (him in)
QA = Deliberately
BP = The Story
OB = Same
AM = Sad
OS = Same
CX = Major (building)
ST = Same

**AR (Poet)** [To-day my Lord of Amiens and myself
Did steal behind him as he lay along

64        THE COMEDIES – WOMEN

Under an oak whose antique root peeps out
Upon the brook that brawls along this wood:
**QA (Sadly)** To the which place a poor sequester'd stag,
That from the hunter's aim had ta'en a hurt,
Did come to languish, and indeed, my lord,
The wretched animal heaved forth such groans
That their discharge did stretch his leathern coat
Almost to bursting, and the big round tears
Coursed one another down his innocent nose
In piteous chase; **QA (Wonderingly)** and thus the hairy fool
Much marked of the melancholy Jaques,
Stood on the extremest verge of the swift brook,
Augmenting it with tears.] *End AF 2*

**Note: This lovely speech addresses both sides of living in the forest and having to hunt for food and use the land in a non-conservative manner. In other words, it is a very early treatise on conservation. The speaker also somewhat anthropomorphizes the wounded deer.**

    *As You Like It* **is basically a play that debates whether it is better to live in the country or in court. This was a popular topic of the period.**

## Three

*Love's Labour's Lost*
Act IV, sc. ii

Berowne—AR—Lover, Magical Child, Poet, Clown

### MONOLOGUE

#### *AF 1*

PG/AC = I Lift/I Confess
QA = Sincerely
BP = The Confession
OB = I desperately want Rosaline's love.
AM = Fear
OS = Rosaline is very wary of my methods of wooing.

# THE COMEDIES – WOMEN

65

CX = Auxiliary
ST = I may lose Rosaline. Heartbreak.

**AR (Poet)** [Thus pour the stars down plagues for perjury.
Can any face of brass hold longer out?] *End AF 1*


## *AF 2*

PG/AC = I Open/I Reveal
QA = Beggingly
BP = The True Woo
OB = Same
AM = Glad (Confessing feels good!)
OS = Same
CX = Building to Major
ST = Same


**AR (Lover)** [Here stand I—lady, dart thy skill at me;
Bruise me with scorn, confound me with a flout;
Thrust thy sharp wit quite through my ignorance;
Cut me to pieces with thy keen conceit,
And I will wish thee never more to dance,
Nor never more in Russian habit wait.
**QA (Humbly)** O, never will I trust to speeches penn'd,
Nor to the motion of a schoolboy's tongue,
Nor never come in vizard to my friend,
Nor woo in rhyme, like a blind harper's song.
**QA (Disgustingly)** Taffeta phrases, silken terms precise,
Three-piled hyperboles, spruce affectation,
Figures pedantical—these summer-flies
Have blown me full of maggot ostentation.
**QA (Promisingly)** I do forswear them, and I here protest
By this white glove, **QA (Prayerfully)** how white the hand God knows,
**QA (Promisingly)** Henceforth my wooing mind shall be express'd
In russet yeas and honest kersey noes.
**(AX) QA (Wholeheartedly)** And, to begin, wench, so God help me, la!
My love to thee is sound, sans crack or flaw.] *End AF 2*

# 66      THE COMEDIES – WOMEN

**Note: Beware of playing the archetypes in this one. Stick to the two playables—Action and Quality of Action.**


## Four

*The Merchant of Venice*
Act I, sc. iii


Shylock—AR—Bully, Child Orphan, Midas, Spoiler

## MONOLOGUE

### *AF 1*

PG/AC = I Penetrate/I Cut (to pieces)
QA = Humbly
BP = The Revenge
OB = I want to put him in his place.
AM = Glad (on cloud nine!)
OS = His armor, his station (above mine).
CX = Major—building slowly
ST = He may decide to kill me.


**AR (Spoiler)** [Signior Antonio, many a time and oft
In the Rialto you have rated me
About my moneys and my usances.
Still have I borne it with a patient shrug,
For sufferance is the badge of all our tribe.
**(AX) QA (Goadingly)** You call me misbeliever, cut-throat dog,
And spit upon my Jewish gaberdine,
And all for use of that which is mine own.
**AR-Bully QA (Businesslikely)** Well then, it now appears you need
    my help:
Go to, then; you come to me, and you say
'Shylock, we would have moneys:' you say so;
**(AX) QA (Accusingly)** You, that did void your rheum upon my
    beard
And foot me as you spurn a stranger cur
Over your threshold: **QA (Mockingly)** Moneys is your suit
What should I say to you? Should I not say

# THE COMEDIES – WOMEN
67

'Hath a dog money? Is it possible
A cur can lend three thousand ducats?' **QA (Humbly-feigned)** Or
Shall I bend low and in a bondman's key,
With bated breath and whispering humbleness, Say this;
'Fair sir, you spit on me on Wednesday last;
**(AX) QA (Angrily)** You spurn'd me such a day; another time
You call'd me dog; and for these courtesies
I'll lend you thus much moneys'?] *End AF 1*

**Note: There is a part of our Technique called inner and outer tempo. We have all experienced this in our lives. There are times when our inner tempo is raging yet we must control it outwardly. Here, in this speech, Shylock takes advantage of his own inner tempo. He is seething inside and yet he controls his qualities to garner the desired reaction from Antonio. Shylock suspects Antonio may not reply negatively in fear of not receiving his request—a loan from Shylock.**

## Five

*The Merchant of Venice*
Act II, sc. ii

Launcelot Gobbo—AR—Clown, Child Dependent, Victim

## SOLILOQUY

### *AF 1*

PG/AC = I Pull/I Search (within)
QA = Boldly
BP = The Weigh In (as if weighing one option to another)
OB = I want to find the right course of Action.
AM = Fear (turns to Glad at end)
OS = My own conscience.
CX = Major (near end)
ST = If I get caught running away I'm done for.

**AR (Victim)** [Certainly my conscience will serve me to run from
this Jew my master. The fiend is at mine elbow and
tempts me saying to me 'Gobbo, Launcelot Gobbo, good

Launcelot,' or 'good Gobbo,' or 'good Launcelot'
'Gobbo, use your legs, take the start, run away.' **PG-I Push, QA (Meekly)** My

**\*Note Polarity (PL) from Boldly to Meekly**

conscience says 'No; take heed,' honest Launcelot;
take heed, honest Gobbo, or, as aforesaid, 'honest
Launcelot Gobbo; do not run; scorn running with thy
heels.' **PG-I Pull, QA (Courageously)** Well, the most courageous
    fiend bids me
pack: 'Via!' says the fiend; 'away!' says the
fiend; 'for the heavens, rouse up a brave mind,'
says the fiend, 'and run.' **PG-I Push, QA (Deflatedly)** Well, my
    conscience,
hanging about the neck of my heart, says very wisely
to me 'My honest friend Launcelot, being an honest
man's son,' or rather an honest woman's son; for,
indeed, my father did something smack, something
grow to, he had a kind of taste; well, my conscience
says 'Launcelot, budge not.' **PG-I Pull, QA (Fiercely)** 'Budge,' says
    the
fiend. **PG-I Push, QA (Embarrassedly)** 'Budge not,' says my
    conscience.
**PG-I Open, QA (Lawyerly)** 'Conscience,' say I, 'you counsel well;'
    'Fiend,'
say I, 'you counsel well:' to be ruled by my
conscience, I should stay with the Jew my master,
who, **QA (Piously)** God bless the mark, **QA (Fearfully)** is a kind of
    devil; and, to
run away from the Jew, I should be ruled by the
fiend, who, saving your reverence, is the devil
himself. **PG-I Push, QA (Distastefully)** Certainly the Jew is the very
    devil
incarnal; and, in my conscience, my conscience is
but a kind of hard conscience, to offer to counsel
me to stay with the Jew. **PG-I Embrace, QA (Made-up-my-mindly)**
    The fiend gives the more
friendly counsel: I will run, fiend; my heels are at your command;
    I will run.] *End AF 1*

# THE COMEDIES – WOMEN

**69**

Note: As you can see we have added another level in this speech by changing PG's frequently. It helps create great Polarity.

As you begin to embody the Technique and eventually (after much repetition) begin to master it, you can incorporate more and more into each speech, scene, or even a single line or word. The Technique has many aspects. Take your time. Use one tool at a time, and then begin to layer.

You'll also note that it is not necessary, in the last two speeches, to create more AF's than the speech needs. It suffices to change PG's and QA's frequently.

## Six

*A Midsummer Night's Dream*
Act I, sc. i

Lysander—AR—Lover, Child Eternal, Victim, Thief

### MONOLOGUE—INTERCUT WITH HERMIA

#### *AF 1*

PG/AC = I Smash/I (can't discover an equal or better synonym ♉)
**QA = Angrily**

Note: Look at the first punctuation. It gives you a hint as to the family of QA's to work on. The first three lines are the thesis statement for the entire speech.

BP = The Puzzle
OB = I want to make sense of this mess.
AM = Mad
OS = The 'sentence' given from Theseus to Hermia.
CX = Major (building to climax on 'Oh, hell!')

Note: In building the climax to 'Oh, hell!' you'll create a nice Rhythmical Wave (RW) as the speech should slow down after and come to its conclusion.

ST = Losing my true love!

**AR (Victim/Lover)** [Ay me! For aught that I could ever read,
Could ever hear by tale or history,

# 70 THE COMEDIES – WOMEN

The course of true love never did run smooth;
**QA (Sorrowfully)** But, either it was different in blood,—
Or else misgraffed in respect of years,—
**QA (Angrily)** Or else it stood upon the choice of friends,—
O hell! To choose love by another's eyes.
**QA (Sympathetically)** Or, if there were a sympathy in choice,
War, death, or sickness did lay siege to it,
Making it momentany as a sound,
Swift as a shadow, short as any dream;
Brief as the lightning in the collied night,
**QA (Angrily)** That, in a spleen, unfolds both heaven and earth,
And ere a man hath power to say 'Behold!'
The jaws of darkness do devour it up:
**QA (Concludingly)** So quick bright things come to confusion.] *End AF 1*

## Seven

*A Midsummer Night's Dream*
Act IV, sc. i

Bottom—AR—Lover, Child Eternal, Dreamer, Victim, Fool

## SOLILOQUY

### *AF 1*

PG/AC = I Open/I Search (for an answer)
QA = Sleepily
BP = The Puzzle
OB = I want to make sense of my dream.
AM = Glad
OS = There is no one here to help.
CX = Major (climaxing near ending)
ST = I may not be able to find the others in time to perform the play . . . tragedy.

**AR (Dreamer)** *(Asleep)* [When my cue comes, call me, and I will answer: my next is, 'Most fair Pyramus.' *(Awakes)* **QA (Confusedly)** Heigh-ho!
Peter Quince! Flute, the bellows-mender! Snout,

# THE COMEDIES – WOMEN

71

the tinker! Starveling! **QA (Angrily)** God's my life, stolen
hence, and left me asleep! **QA (Profoundly)** I have had a most rare
vision. I have had a dream, past the wit of man to
say what dream it was: **QA (Dismissedly)** man is but an ass, if he go
about to expound this dream. **QA (Searchingly)** Methought I
    was—there
is no man can tell what. Methought I was,—and
methought I had,—**QA (Firmly)** but man is but a patched fool, if
he will offer to say what methought I had. **QA (Unbelievingly)** The
    eye
of man hath not heard, the ear of man hath not
seen, man's hand is not able to taste, his tongue
to conceive, nor his heart to report, what my dream
was. **QA (Brilliantly)** I will get Peter Quince to write a ballad of
this dream: it shall be called Bottom's Dream,
because it hath no bottom; and I will sing it in the
latter end of a play, before the duke:
**QA (Proclaimingly)** peradventure, to make it the more gracious,
    I shall
sing it at her death.] *End AF 1*

**Note: It's time to remind the reader/actor/teacher that these QA's and
PG's have not come to me intellectually. They have occurred organically
by Doing—on my feet. It is a good thing to try these choices as written.
You'll find it to be a good exercise, but it will not be an organic process.
Find your own choices—on your feet!**

## Eight

*Much Ado About Nothing*
Act II, sc. iii

Benedick—AR—Lover, Child Eternal, Poet, Liberator, Judge

## SOLILOQUY

### *AF 1*

PG/AC = I Open/I Ponder
QA = Bewilderedly
BP = The Treatise

OB = I want to come to terms with this dilemma.
AM = Bad

**(Note: Benedick is removing himself from the situation and putting the absent Claudio in his place. Therefore, being removed, he feels bad and not sad, for Claudio.)**

OS = Claudio is my friend—how can I help him?
CX = Auxiliary
ST = Loss of my friend!

**AR (Judge)** [I do much wonder that one man, seeing how much
another man is a fool when he dedicates his
behaviors to love, will, after he hath laughed at
such shallow follies in others, become the argument
of his own scorn by failing in love: and such a man
is Claudio. **QA (Militarily)** I have known when there was no music
with him but the drum and the fife; **QA (Longingly)** and now had he
rather hear the tabour and the pipe: **QA (Proudly)** I have known
when he would have walked ten mile a-foot to see a
good armour; **QA (Pitifully)** and now will he lie ten nights awake,
carving the fashion of a new doublet. **QA (Firmly)** He was wont to
speak plain and to the purpose, like an honest man
and a soldier; **QA (Bitterly)** and now is he turned orthography; his
words are a very fantastical banquet, just so many
strange dishes. **QA (Searchingly)** May I be so converted and see with
these eyes? I cannot tell; I think not: **QA (Swearingly)** I will not
be sworn, but love may transform me to an oyster; but
I'll take my oath on it, till he have made an oyster
of me, he shall never make me such a fool.] *End AF 1*

### *AF 2*

PG/AC = I Pull/I Struggle (with the issue)
QA = Admiringly
BP = The Sorting Out
OB = Same
AM = Glad
OS = Same

# THE COMEDIES – WOMEN

73

CX = Major (at ending)
ST = Same

[One woman is fair, **QA (Conclusively)** yet I am well; **QA (Truth-fully)** another is wise, **QA
(Conclusively)** yet I am well; **QA (Judgementally, in a good way)** another virtuous, **QA
(Conclusively)** yet I am well; **QA (Absolutely)** but till all graces be in one woman, one woman
shall not come in my grace. Rich she shall be, that's certain; **QA (Truthfully)** wise,
or I'll none; **(QA (Judgementally, in a good way)** virtuous, or I'll never cheapen her;
**QA (Admiringly)** fair, or I'll never look on her; **QA (Mildly)** mild, or come not
near me; **QA (Regally)** noble, or not I for an angel; **(Count-offedly, as in a list)** of good
discourse, an excellent musician, and her hair shall
be **QA (Who-cares-ed-ly)** of what colour it please God. QA (Surprisingly) Ha! the prince and
Monsieur Love! I will hide me in the arbour.] *End AF 2*

**Note: This is a great example of Veiling. (See exercises.) It's interesting Benedick is Veiling his own feelings from himself.**

## Nine

*Twelfth Night*
Act I, sc. i

Orsino—AR—Lover, Child Wounded, Poet, King (Duke,) Seeker, Addict

### MONOLOGUE

### *AF 1*

PG/AC = I Open/I Wax (poetic)
QA = Happily
BP = The Poem

74 THE COMEDIES – WOMEN

OB = I want to enlighten those around me.
AM = Glad and Sad
OS = It may fall on deaf ears.
CX = Auxiliary
ST = The love of life, Olivia, and love itself may be lost.

**AR (Poet/Lover)** [If music be the food of love, play on;
Give me excess of it, that, surfeiting,
**QA (Sadly)** The appetite may sicken, and so die.
**QA (Joyfully)** That strain again! It had a dying fall:
O, it came o'er my ear like the sweet sound,
That breathes upon a bank of violets,
Stealing and giving odour!] *End AF 1*

## *AF 2*

PG/AC = I Close/I Shut Down
QA = Woefully
BP = The Giving In
OB = Same
AM = Sad
OS = Same
CX = Auxiliary
ST = Same

**Note the continuation of the line from AF 1. . .**

[Enough; no more:
'Tis not so sweet now as it was before.
O spirit of love! how quick and fresh art thou,
That, notwithstanding thy capacity
Receiveth as the sea, nought enters there,
Of what validity and pitch soe'er,
But falls into abatement and low price,
Even in a minute: so full of shapes is fancy
That it alone is high fantastical.] *End AF 2*

**Cut to. . .**

# THE COMEDIES – WOMEN

## *AF 3*

PG/AC = I Embrace/I Confess
QA = Longingly
BP = The Real Deal
OB = Same
AM = Fear (as she does not return my love)
OS = Same
CX = Major
ST = Same

*AF 3* **(AX)** [O, when mine eyes did see Olivia first,
Methought she purged the air of pestilence!
That instant was I turn'd into a hart;
And my desires, like fell and cruel hounds,
E'er since pursue me.
*Enter VALENTINE*
**QA (Hopefully) (AX)** How now! What news from her?] *End AF 3*

## Ten

*The Two Gentlemen of Verona*
Act II, sc. iii

Launce—AR—Clown, Child Eternal, Trickster

## SOLILOQUY

### *AF 1*

PG/AC = I Throw/I Vomit (this out)
QA = Weepingly
BP = The Parting
OB = I want the folks to take my side.
AM = Sad
OS = Crab is unrelenting.
CX = Auxiliary to Major
ST = The folks will side with Crab.

# 76

## THE COMEDIES – WOMEN

**AR (Clown)** [Nay, 'twill be this hour ere I have done weeping;
all the kind of the Launces have this very fault. I
have received my proportion, like the prodigious
son, and am going with Sir Proteus to the Imperial's
court.] *End AF 1*


**Note: The first AF could be cut for length.**


## *AF 2*

PG/AC = I Wring/I Tug
QA = Sourly
BP = The Pity Me Speech
OB = Same
AM = Mad and Sad
OS = Same
CX = Same
ST = Same


**AM (Mad)** [I think Crab, my dog, be the sourest-natured
dog that lives: **AM (Sad) QA (Sorrowfully)** my mother weeping,
   **AM (Mad) QA**
**(Embarrassedly)** my father wailing, **(AM Sad) QA (Hurtfully)** my
   sister crying, **AM (Mad)**
**QA (Exasperatedly)** our maid howling, **AM (Sad) QA (Unbelievably)** our cat wringing her
hands, and all our house in a great perplexity, **(AX) AM (Mad) QA
   (Perplexedly)** yet did not
this cruel-hearted cur shed one tear: **PG (I Smash) AM (Sad) QA
   (Woefully)** he is a stone, a
very pebble stone, and has no more pity in him than a dog: **AM
   (Mad) QA (Brazzenly)** a Jew
would have wept to have seen our parting; **PG (I Embrace) QA
   (Lovingly) AM (Sad)** why, my
grandam, having no eyes, look you, wept herself blind at my
parting. **AM (Mad) PG (I Push/I Press) QA (Teacherly)** Nay, I'll
   show you the manner of it.
This shoe is my father: **QA (Wisely)** no, this left shoe is my father:
**QA (Frustratedly)** no, no, this left shoe is my mother: nay, that

# THE COMEDIES – WOMEN

cannot be so neither: **QA (Surely)** yes, it is so, it is so, it
hath the worser sole. This shoe, with the hole in
it, is my mother, and this my father; **(AX)** a vengeance
on't! There 'tis: **QA (Commandingly)** now, sit, **QA (Patiently)** this
   staff is my
sister, for, look you, **QA (Lovingly)** she is as white as a lily and
as small as a wand: **QA (Respectfully)** this hat is Nan, our maid:
   **QA (Boldly)** I
am the dog: **QA (Frustratedly)** no, the dog is himself, and I am the
dog—Oh! The dog is me, and I am myself; ay, so,
so. **QA (Teacherly)** Now come I to my father; Father, your blessing:
now should not the shoe speak a word for weeping:
now should I kiss my father; well, he weeps on. Now
come I to my mother: **QA (Angrily)** O, that she could speak now
like a wood woman! **QA (Sorrowfully)** Well, I kiss her; why, there
'tis; here's my mother's breath up and down. **QA (Teacherly)** Now
come I to my sister; **QA (Tearfully)** mark the moan she makes. **PG**
   **(I Open) (I Pour—out my heart)**
**QA (Pitifully)** Now the dog all this while sheds not a tear nor speaks a
word; but see how I lay the dust with my tears.] *End AF 2*

**Note: What a wild ride on a RW this speech can be! It is the changes
in the QA's that really sets this speech, and you, apart. Don't attempt
this speech in an audition unless you've really done your homework. It
is a speech that is commonly attempted and most of the time the actor
rants on and on in anger with no variances in PG and QA.**

**Note: From this point I will not identify AX's. Find them by the QA's
and identify them for yourself. It's only in this way you will find the
major climax of each speech. When you find the climax rehearse it first
and build your RW around it.**

### End Chapter Three

Other speeches to consider from the Comedies (Index of First Lines)

1.  *As You Like It*
    Act II, sc. vii
    Jaques—'All the world's a stage. . . '

78 THE COMEDIES – WOMEN

2. *As You Like It*
   Act III, sc. v
   Phebe—'I would not be thy executioner. . . '

3. *The Comedy of Errors*
   Act II, sc. ii
   Adriana—'Ay; ay, Antipholus, look strange and frown. . . '

4. *The Merchant of Venice*
   Act III, sc. i
   Shylock—'To bait fish withal. . . '

5. *A Midsummer Night's Dream*
   Act I, sc. i
   Theseus—'Either to die the death, or to abjure. . . '

6. *A Midsummer Night's Dream*
   Act II, sc. i
   Oberon—'My gentle Puck, come hither. . . ' through 'Ere the levia-
   than can swim a league. . . '

7. *A Midsummer Night's Dream*
   Act III, sc. ii
   Puck—'My mistress with a monster is in love. . . '

8. *Much Ado About Nothing*
   Act II, sc. iii
   Benedick—'This can be no trick. . . '

9. *The Taming of the Shrew*
   Act IV, sc. i
   Petruchio—'Thus have I politicly begun my reign. . . '

# Chapter Four

# THE TRAGEDIES – WOMEN

## One

*Antony and Cleopatra*
Act I, sc. v

Cleopatra—AR—Queen, Child Eternal, Lover, Seductress

### MONOLOGUE

### *AF 1*

PG/AC = I Embrace/I Devour (the thought of Antony)
QA = Lonely
BP = The Double Entendre
OB = I want Antony . . . NOW!
AM = Glad
OS = Antony is in Rome.
CX = Major
ST = I am empty without Antony. How can I be all that I need to be
without completeness?

**AR (Lover)** [O Charmian,
Where think'st thou he is now? Stands he, or sits he?
Or does he walk? **QA (Lustily)** Or is he on his horse?
O happy horse, to bear the weight of Antony!
**QA (Challengingly)** Do bravely, horse, for wot'st thou whom thou
movest?

**QA (Admiringly)** The demi-Atlas of this earth, the arm
And burgonet of men.
**QA (Hornily)** He's speaking now,
Or murmuring 'Where's my serpent of old Nile?'
For so he calls me: now I feed myself
With most delicious poison.] *End AF 1*

### AF 2

PG/AC = I Close/I Reflect
QA = Sadly
BP = The Turning Inward
OB = I want Antony. I want to be validated.
AM = Sad
OS = Same
CX = Auxiliary
ST = Same

**AR (Queen)** [Think on me,
That am with Phoebus' amorous pinches black,
And wrinkled deep in time? **QA (Bitterly)** Broad-fronted Caesar,
When thou wast here above the ground, I was
A morsel for a monarch: and great Pompey
Would stand and make his eyes grow in my brow;
There would he anchor his aspect and die
With looking on his life.] *End AF 2*

**Note: Please take the time to research the double entendres in AF 1.
You will find delight in the meanings, and your findings will offer great
insight as to the playfulness of Cleopatra.**

## Two

*Antony and Cleopatra*
Act IV, sc. xv

Cleopatra—AR—Queen, Child Eternal, Lover, Seductress

# THE TRAGEDIES – WOMEN

# MONOLOGUE

## *AF 1*

PG/AC = I Embrace/I Enfold
QA = Challengingly
BP = The Hope
OB = I want Antony to live.
AM = Fear
OS = I cannot overcome death.
CX = Auxiliary
ST = The world is no longer livable without Antony.

**AR (Lover)** [Noblest of men, woo't die?
Hast thou no care of me? Shall I abide
In this dull world, which in thy absence is
No better than a sty? (*MARK ANTONY dies*)] *End AF 1*

## *AF 2*

PG/AC = I Lift/I Testify
QA = Mournfully
BP = The Testament
OB = I want to revere a giant among men!
AM = Sad
OS = Same
CX = Major (Ebbing and flowing with punctuation)
ST = Same

**AR (Lover—Queen)** [O, see, my women—
The crown o' the earth doth melt. **QA (Proudly)** My lord!
**QA (Defiantly)** O, wither'd is the garland of the war,
The soldier's pole is fall'n; young boys and girls
Are level now with men; the odds is gone,
And there is nothing left remarkable
Beneath the visiting moon!
**QA (Pitifully)** No more but e'en a woman, and commanded
By such poor passion as the maid that milks

And does the meanest chares. **QA (Cursingly)** It were for me
To throw my sceptre at the injurious gods,
To tell them that this world did equal theirs
Till they had stol'n our jewel. **QA (Philosophically)** All's but naught-
Patience is scottish, and impatience does
Become a dog that's mad; then is it sin
To rush into the secret house of death,
Ere death dare come to us? **QA (Queenly)** How do you, women?
What, what! Good cheer! Why, how now, Charmian?
My noble girls! Ah, women, women. Look!
**QA (Woefully)** Our lamp is spent, it's out! **QA (Queenly)** Good sirs,
    take heart.
We'll bury him; **QA (Proudly)** and then, what's brave, what's noble,
Let's do it after the high Roman fashion,
And make death proud to take us. **QA (Emptily)** Come, away-
This case of that huge spirit now is cold.
**QA (Decidedly)** Ah, women, women! Come; we have no friend
But resolution and the briefest end.] *End AF 2*

**Note: It's very easy to fall into the trap of playing emotion in this speech. Cleopatra reveres and loves Antony too much to allow his death to be cheapened by becoming a blubbering idiot. Stick with your Actions and Qualities.**

## Three

*Hamlet*
Act II, sc. i

Ophelia—AR—Lover, Child Dependent, Prostitute, Victim

### MONOLOGUE

### *AF 1*

PG/AC = I Open/I Reveal
QA = Carefully
BP = The Scary Truth
OB = I want my father to relieve my fears.

## THE TRAGEDIES – WOMEN

AM = Fear
OS = If my love is truly mad how can my fears be relieved?
CX = Major
ST = Depending on what my father says I may be heartbroken.

**AR (Victim)** [My lord, as I was sewing in my closet,
Lord Hamlet, with his doublet all unbraced
No hat upon his head, his stockings foul'd,
Ungarter'd, and down-gyved to his ankles,
**QA (Fearfully)** Pale as his shirt; his knees knocking each other,
And with a look so piteous in purport
As if he had been loosed out of hell
To speak of horrors—he comes before me.
**QA (Helplessly)** He took me by the wrist and held me hard.
**QA (Pitifully)** Then goes he to the length of all his arm,
And, with his other hand thus o'er his brow,
He falls to such perusal of my face
As he would draw it. **QA (Longingly)** Long stay'd he so;
**QA (Fearfully)** At last, a little shaking of mine arm,
And thrice his head thus waving up and down,
He raised a sigh so piteous and profound
As it did seem to shatter all his bulk
And end his being. That done, he lets me go:
**QA (Puzzlingly)** And, with his head over his shoulder turn'd,
He seem'd to find his way without his eyes,
For out o' doors he went without their helps,
And, to the last, bended their light on me.] *End AF 1*

**Note: In this speech notice the Polarity (PL) between Qualities of Action. This is a straightforward speech so the Qualities create the RW. Whatever Qualities you find please be sure to incorporate PL.**

## Four

*Hamlet*
Act III, sc. i

Ophelia—AR—Lover, Child Dependent, Prostitute, Victim

# SOLILOQUY

## *AF 1*

PG/AC = I Wring/I Wrench (Inside)
QA = Gut Wrenchingly
BP = The Proof
OB = I want to face the truth.
AM = Mad
OS = The truth is hard to bear.
CX = Major
ST = What is to become of me? I have given all to Hamlet.


**AR (Lover)** [O, what a noble mind is here o'erthrown!
**QA (Courtly)** The courtier's, **QA (Soldierly)** soldier's, **QA (Scholarly)** scholar's,
**QA (Admiringly)** eye, **QA (Lovingly)** tongue, **QA (Fiercely)** sword;
**QA (Royally)** The expectancy and rose of the fair state,
**QA (Proudly)** The glass of fashion and the mould of form,
**QA (Put on a Pedestal-ly)** The observed of all observers, **AM (Sad)** **QA (Sorrowfully)** quite,
quite down.
**QA (Dejectedly)** And I, of ladies most deject and wretched,
That suck'd the honey of his music vows,
Now see that noble and most sovereign reason,
Like sweet bells jangled, out of tune and harsh;
That unmatch'd form and feature of blown youth
Blasted with ecstasy: **QA (Woefully)** O, woe is me,
To have seen what I have seen, see what I see!] *End AF 1*


**Note: The number of QA's in this speech may seem somewhat overboard. Yet, consider that, when you have a list as we have here, unless you change QA's with each item you are not truly imagining the specificity of the item. After all an orange is not an apple just as a 'soldier' is not a 'scholar.' It is a short speech so no need to rush through the images.**

**Take your time.**

THE TRAGEDIES – WOMEN                    85

# Five

*Hamlet*
Act IV, sc. vii

Gertrude—AR—Queen, Child Devine, Lover, Victim, Mother

## MONOLOGUE

### *AF 1*

PG/AC = I Embrace/I Inform
QA = Difficultly
BP = The Worst News
OB = I want Laertes to hear the news from me.
AM = Sad
OS = Laerte's anger
CX = Major
ST = Laertes may blame my son and blood will follow.


**AR (Mother)** [One woe doth tread upon another's heel,
So fast they follow; your sister's drown'd, Laertes.
**QA (Descriptively)** There is a willow grows aslant a brook,
That shows his hoar leaves in the glassy stream.
There with fantastic garlands did she come
Of crow-flowers, **QA (Confusedly)** nettles, **QA (Prettily)** daisies,
    **QA (Confusedly)** and long
purples
That liberal shepherds give a grosser name,
**QA (Sadly)** But our cold maids do dead men's fingers call them.
**QA (Difficultly)** There, on the pendent boughs her coronet weeds
Clambering to hang, an envious sliver broke;
When down her weedy trophies and herself
Fell in the weeping brook. **QA (Hold-back-ed-ly)** Her clothes
    spread wide;
And, mermaid-like, awhile they bore her up,
Which time she chanted snatches of old tunes
As one incapable of her own distress,

86 THE TRAGEDIES – WOMEN

Or like a creature native and indued
Unto that element. **QA (Sorrowfully)** But long it could not be
Till that her garments, heavy with their drink,
Pull'd the poor wretch from her melodious lay
To muddy death.] *End AF 1*

**Note: Take care with this monologue. You have to make some choices that will affect your QA's. Did Gertrude try to save Ophelia from drowning or was she a bystander? Is Gertrude mainly trying to protect Hamlet or is she chiefly saddened by the event? You have to make some decisions about the Queen's morality and through-line. Enjoy.**

## Six

*Julius Caesar*
Act II, sc. i

Portia—AR—Lover, Child Devine, Victim

## MONOLOGUE

### *AF1*

PG/AC = I Penetrate/I Probe
QA = Impatiently
BP = The Inquiry
OB = I want to learn what's troubling my husband.
AM = Fear
OS = Brutus can be stubborn.
CX = Major
ST = There may be trouble brewing and Brutus in danger.

**AR (Victim)** [Y'have ungently, Brutus,
Stole from my bed. And yesternight, at supper,
You suddenly arose, and walk'd about,
Musing and sighing, with your arms across,
And when I ask'd you what the matter was,
You stared upon me with ungentle looks.

# THE TRAGEDIES – WOMEN

**QA (Urgently)** I urged you further; **QA (Wonderingly)** then you
    scratch'd your head,
**QA (Fearfully)** And too impatiently stamp'd with your foot;
**QA (Insistently)** Yet I insisted, yet you answer'd not,
**QA (Hurtfully)** But, with an angry wafture of your hand,
Gave sign for me to leave you. **QA (Dutifully)** So I did;
Fearing to strengthen that impatience
Which seem'd too much enkindled, and withal
Hoping it was but an effect of humour,
Which sometime hath his hour with every man.
**QA (Motherly)** It will not let you eat, nor talk, nor sleep,
And could it work so much upon your shape
As it hath much prevail'd on your condition,
I should not know you, Brutus. **QA (Pleadingly)** Dear my lord,
Make me acquainted with your cause of grief.] *End AF 1*

**Note: This is part of a much longer speech. I would suggest you look
at the entire speech for full content or if the other parts more suit
your purpose. This particular part should run just over a minute (for
audition information).**

## Seven

*Julius Caesar*
Act II, sc. ii

Calphurnia—AR—Lover, Child Devine, Queen, Matriarch

### MONOLOGUE

### *AF 1*

PG/AC = I Pull/I Warn
QA = I Demand
BP = The Warning
OB = I want Caesar to be safe.
AM = Fear
OS = Caesar is Caesar and listens only to himself.

88      THE TRAGEDIES – WOMEN

CX = Major
ST = Something terrible may happen to Caesar if he goes out.

**AR (Queen)** [What mean you, Caesar? Think you to walk forth?
You shall not stir out of your house to-day.
**PG (I Push) QA (Firmly)** Caesar, I never stood on ceremonies,
Yet now they fright me. **PG (I Pull) QA (Revealingly)** There is one
    within,
Besides the things that we have heard and seen,
Recounts most horrid sights seen by the watch.
**QA (Frightfully)** A lioness hath whelped in the streets,
And graves have yawn'd, and yielded up their dead;
Fierce fiery warriors fought upon the clouds
In ranks and squadrons and right form of war,
Which drizzled blood upon the Capitol;
The noise of battle hurtled in the air,
Horses did neigh, and dying men did groan,
And ghosts did shriek and squeal about the streets.
**QA (Hopelessly)** O Caesar! These things are beyond all use,
And I do fear them.] *End AF 1*

**Note: Identify the AX's and take the climax on the strong caesura near the end. It's a great build if you don't begin too high on the QA of 'Frightfully.'**

## Eight

*King Lear*
Act I, sc. iv

Goneril—AR—Lover, Child Wounded, Victim, Princess, Seduc-
    tress

### MONOLOGUE

#### *AF 1*

PG/AC = I Wring/I Squeeze
QA = Confront-ed-ly

THE TRAGEDIES – WOMEN 89

BP = The Demand
OB = I want my house back!
AM = Mad
OS = My father hates giving in to an kind of reason.
CX = Major
ST = The King has too much power with all of these knights.

**AR (Victim)** [Not only, sir, this your all-licensed fool,
But other of your insolent retinue
Do hourly carp and quarrel; breaking forth
In rank and not-to-be endured riots. **PG (I Close) QA (Hurtfully)**
    Sir,
I had thought, by making this well known unto you,
To have found a safe redress; but now grow fearful,
By what yourself too late have spoke and done.
**PG (I Embrace) QA (Patiently)** This admiration, sir, is much o' the
    savour
Of other your new pranks. I do beseech you
To understand my purposes aright:
**QA (Lovingly)** As you are old and reverend, you should be wise.
Here do you keep a hundred knights and squires;
Men so disorder'd, so debosh'd and bold,
That this our court, infected with their manners,
Shows like a riotous inn: **PG (I Push) QA (Chidingly)** epicurism
    and lust
Make it more like a tavern or a brothel
Than a graced palace. The shame itself doth speak
For instant remedy. **PG (I Embrace) QA (Reasonably)** Be then
    desired
By her, that else will take the thing she begs,
A little to disquantity your train;
And the remainder, that shall still depend,
To be such men as may besort your age,
And know themselves and you.] *End AF 1*


**Note: It's easy to fall into playing mad from the beginning of this monologue. Goneril is cunning, and she uses her wits to try to get what she wants. Change AC's and QA's frequently, and use Polarity.**

# Nine

*Macbeth*
Act I, sc. v

Lady Macbeth—AR—Lover, Child Magical, Seductress, Bully, Vampire

## SOLILOQUY

### *AF 1*

PG/AC = I Open/I Profess
QA = Resolutely
BP = The Summoning
OB = I want help to be successful.
AM = Fear
OS = Being alone in the quest.
CX = Major
ST = I have set myself on a dangerous course.

**AR (Vampire)** [The raven himself is hoarse
That croaks the fatal entrance of Duncan
Under my battlements. **QA (Invitingly)** Come, you spirits
That tend on mortal thoughts, unsex me here,
And fill me from the crown to the toe top-full
Of direst cruelty! **QA (Demandingly)** Make thick my blood;
Stop up the access and passage to remorse,
That no compunctious visitings of nature
Shake my fell purpose, nor keep peace between
The effect and it! **QA (Seductively)** Come to my woman's breasts,
And take my milk for gall, you murdering ministers,
Wherever in your sightless substances
You wait on nature's mischief! **QA (Conjuringly)** Come, thick
   night,
And pall thee in the dunnest smoke of hell,
That my keen knife see not the wound it makes,
Nor heaven peep through the blanket of the dark,
To cry 'Hold, hold!'] *End AF 1*

# THE TRAGEDIES – WOMEN

91

**Note: The Elizabethans wholeheartedly believed in demonic spirits. You have to buy into this idea to make the stakes high and ground the speech in reality.**

## Ten

*Macbeth*
Act I, sc. vii

Lady Macbeth—AR—Lover, Child Magical, Seductress, Bully, Vampire, Mother

### MONOLOGUE

#### *AF 1*

PG/AC = I Push/I Challenge
QA = Bullishly
BP = The Gauntlet
OB = I want Macbeth to follow through.
AM = Mad
OS = Macbeth has changed his mind.
CX = Auxiliary
ST = The Throne!

**AR (Bully)** [Was the hope drunk
Wherein you dress'd yourself? Hath it slept since?
And wakes it now, to look so green and pale
At what it did so freely? From this time
Such I account thy love. Art thou afeard
To be the same in thine own act and valour
As thou art in desire? Wouldst thou have that
Which thou esteem'st the ornament of life,
And live a coward in thine own esteem,
Letting 'I dare not' wait upon 'I would,'
Like the poor cat i' the adage?
**QA (Challengingly)** When you durst do it, then you were a man;

**Note: See if you can challenge Macbeth in a manner other than bullishly or harshly. Use Polarity.**

And, to be more than what you were, you would
Be so much more the man. Nor time nor place
Did then adhere, and yet you would make both.
They have made themselves, and that their fitness now
Does unmake you.] *End AF 1*

## *AF 2*

PG/AC = I Open/I Reveal
QA = Creepily
BP = The Call to Arms
OB = Same
AM = Same
OS = Same
CX = Same
ST = Same

**AR (Vampire)** [I have given suck, and know
How tender 'tis to love the babe that milks me:
I would, while it was smiling in my face,
Have pluck'd my nipple from his boneless gums,
And dash'd the brains out, had I so sworn as you
Have done to this.] *End AF 2* **Note missing feet as Macbeth has a line here.**

## *AF 3*

PG/AC = I Embrace/I Seduce
QA = Seductively
BP = The Closing Argument
OB = Same
AM = Glad
OS = Same
CX = Major
ST = Same

**AR (Seductress)** [But screw your courage to the sticking-place,
And we'll not fail. When Duncan is asleep—

THE TRAGEDIES – WOMEN                    93

Whereto the rather shall his day's hard journey
Soundly invite him—his two chamberlains
Will I with wine and wassail so convince
That memory, the warder of the brain,
Shall be a fume, and the receipt of reason
A limbeck only: when in swinish sleep
Their drenched natures lie as in a death,
What cannot you and I perform upon
The unguarded Duncan? What not put upon
His spongy officers, who shall bear the guilt
Of our great quell?] *End AF 3*

**Note: Finding different ways to seduce Macbeth is key to AF 3. It
needs to get 'hotter' as it moves forward. The speech, as cut, is far
too long for an audition. It is, however, an excellent piece to work on
as almost the entire character of Lady Macbeth is revealed in this one
monologue. Perhaps you can find a way to cut it for an audition while
maintaining the scansion and archetypes.**

## Eleven

*Othello*
Act IV, sc. iii

Emelia—AR—Servant, Child Nature, Teacher, Companion,
  Lover

## MONOLOGUE

### *AF 1*

PG/AC = I Lift/I Instruct
QA = Opinionatedly
BP = The Fault
OB = I want Desdemona to grow up a bit.
AM = Glad
OS = Desdemona is naïve.
CX = Major
ST = Desdemona's ultimate happiness in her marriage.

## 94    THE TRAGEDIES – WOMEN

**AR (Teacher/Companion)** [But I do think it is their husbands'
   faults
If wives do fall. **QA (Hatefully)** Say that they slack their duties,
And pour our treasures into foreign laps;
**QA (Wonderingly)** Or else break out in peevish jealousies,
Throwing restraint upon us; **QA (Hurtfully)** or say they strike us,
**QA (Begrudgingly)** Or scant our former having in despite;
**QA (Confessedly)** Why, we have galls, **QA (Truthfully)** and though
   we have some grace,
**QA (By-God-ed-ly)** Yet have we some revenge. **QA (Advisedly)** Let
   husbands know
Their wives have sense like them: they see and smell
And have their palates both for sweet and sour,
As husbands have. **QA (Quizzically)** What is it that they do
When they change us for others? Is it sport?
**QA (Decidedly)** I think it is: **QA (Quizzically)** and doth affection
   breed it?
**QA (Decidedly)** I think it doth: **QA (Blamingly)** is't frailty that thus
   errs?
**QA (Decidedly)** It is so too: **QA (Closingly)** and have not we
   affections,
Desires for sport, and frailty, as men have?
Then let them use us well: else let them know,
The ills we do, their ills instruct us so.] *End AF 1*

**Note: Emilia's monologue must be active. Refrain from sitting for this,
or really any speech, for anything other than the briefest of times. In
the scene, Desdemona is preparing for bed and Emilia is assisting her.
You can't really mime these Actions. So—the main task is to make the
speech active through the PG's and QA's. Don't be afraid, as always, to
inject different PG's where you may find them. Remember, this is the
way I am building the work. You have an obligation to find your own
journey via this template.**

## Twelve

*Romeo and Juliet*
Act III, sc. ii

Juliet—AR—Lover, Child Eternal, Victim, Princess

# SOLILOQUY

## *AF 1*

PG/AC = I Embrace/I Plead
QA = Anxiously
BP = The Anticipated Event
OB = I want Romeo to take me.
AM = Glad
OS = Time is of the essence.
CX = Major (carefully building)
ST = Romeo must not be seen or suspected or it will all be for naught.


**AR (Lover)** [Gallop apace, you fiery-footed steeds,
Towards Phoebus' lodging: such a wagoner
As Phaethon would whip you to the west,
And bring in cloudy night immediately.
**QA (Beggingly)** Spread thy close curtain, love-performing night,
That runaway's eyes may wink and Romeo
Leap to these arms, untalk'd of and unseen.
**QA (Smartly)** Lovers can see to do their amorous rites
By their own beauties; or, if love be blind,
It best agrees with night. **QA (Prayerfully)** Come, civil night,
Thou sober-suited matron, all in black,
And learn me how to lose a winning match,
Play'd for a pair of stainless maidenhoods.
Hood my unmann'd blood, bating in my cheeks,
With thy black mantle; till strange love, grown bold,
Think true love acted simple modesty.
**QA (Poetically)** Come, night; come, Romeo; come, thou day in
  night;
For thou wilt lie upon the wings of night
Whiter than new snow on a raven's back
Come, gentle night, come, loving, black-brow'd night,
Give me my Romeo; and, when he shall die,
Take him and cut him out in little stars,
And he will make the face of heaven so fine
That all the world will be in love with night
And pay no worship to the garish sun.
**QA (Impatiently)** O, I have bought the mansion of a love,

But not possess'd it, and, though I am sold,
Not yet enjoy'd: so tedious is this day
As is the night before some festival
To an impatient child that hath new robes
And may not wear them. **QA (Excitedly)** O, here comes my nurse,
And she brings news; and every tongue that speaks
But Romeo's name speaks heavenly eloquence.] *End AF 1*

**Note: Juliet is obviously excited to finally be bedded by Romeo. Her subjective atmosphere is Glad while the objective atmosphere is Fear. We have all felt this way in some situation or another. It is the struggle with the atmospheres that is most interesting. Decide where Glad overcomes the Fear and you will find the major climax.**

## APPLICATION OF THE MICHAEL CHEKHOV TECHNIQUE TO SHAKESPEARE'S MONOLOGUES AND SOLILOQUIES

### *THE TRAGEDIES-MEN*

## One

*Antony and Cleopatra*
Act II, sc. ii

Enobarbus—AR—Warrior, Child Dependent, Storyteller

### MONOLOGUE

### *AF 1*

PG/AC = I Lift/I Unveil
QA = Poetically
BP = The Tale of Cleopatra's Arrival
OB = I want everyone to understand what we're up against.
AM = Fear
OS = The Direness of the Situation
CX = Auxiliary

# THE TRAGEDIES – WOMEN

97

ST = Rome could come to war with itself between Antony and
Caesar.

**AR (Storyteller)** [I will tell you.
The barge she sat in, like a burnish'd throne,
Burn'd on the water: the poop was beaten gold;
Purple the sails, and so perfumed that
The winds were love-sick with them; the oars were silver,
Which to the tune of flutes kept stroke, and made
The water which they beat to follow faster,
As amorous of their strokes. **QA (Admiringly)** For her own
person,
It beggar'd all description: she did lie
In her pavilion—cloth-of-gold of tissue—
O'er-picturing that Venus where we see
The fancy outwork nature: **QA (Condescendingly)** on each side her
Stood pretty dimpled boys, like smiling Cupids,
With divers-colour'd fans, whose wind did seem
To glow the delicate cheeks which they did cool,
And what they undid did.
**QA (Regally)** Her gentlewomen, like the Nereides,
So many mermaids, tended her i' the eyes,
And made their bends adornings: **QA (Admiringly)** at the helm
A seeming mermaid steers: the silken tackle
Swell with the touches of those flower-soft hands,
That yarely frame the office. **QA (Fearfully)** From the barge
A strange invisible perfume hits the sense
Of the adjacent wharfs. The city cast
Her people out upon her; and Antony,
Enthroned i' the market-place, did sit alone,
Whistling to the air; which, but for vacancy,
Had gone to gaze on Cleopatra too,
And made a gap in nature.
**QA (Bewilderedly)** Upon her landing, Antony sent to her,
Invited her to supper: she replied,
It should be better he became her guest;
Which she entreated: our courteous Antony,

98 THE TRAGEDIES – WOMEN

Whom ne'er the word of 'No' woman heard speak,
Being barber'd ten times o'er, goes to the feast,
And for his ordinary pays his heart
For what his eyes eat only.] *End AF 1*

**Enobarbus is a loyal lieutenant to Antony. It is important to know that the people he is talking to have a mixture of atmospheres—Mad and Fear. His purpose, in this speech, is to report clearly and concisely. Yet, he is dealing with these atmospheres as well within himself. His struggle to contain his subjective atmosphere is what is most interesting about this speech. Careful with tempo on this one. It should be slow and methodical.**

**In longer speeches such as this it is important to remember that you can, when rehearsing, physically reinvest in the PG. You can always insert more PG's if you feel the need. I find it unnecessary to change the Action unless it is truly called for. QA changes most often suffice.**

## Two

*Coriolanus*
Act IV, sc. v

Coriolanus—AR—Warrior, Child Eternal, Tyrant, Dreamer, Politician

## MONOLOGUE

### *AF 1*

PG/AC = I Open/I Apologize
QA = Sincerely
BP = The Apology
OB = I want the help of Tullus Aufidius to conquer Rome.
AM = Fear
OS = I have defeated the Volcians five times. They could be pissed-off.
CX = Auxiliary
ST = They may decide to kill me now.

**AR (Politician)** [My name is Caius Marcius, who hath done
To thee particularly and to all the Volsces
Great hurt and mischief; thereto witness may
My surname, Coriolanus. The painful service,
The extreme dangers and the drops of blood
Shed for my thankless country are requited
But with that surname; a good memory,
And witness of the malice and displeasure
Which thou shouldst bear me. Only that name remains:
**QA (Hurtfully)** The cruelty and envy of the people,
Permitted by our dastard nobles, who
Have all forsook me, hath devour'd the rest;
And suffer'd me by the voice of slaves to be
Whoop'd out of Rome.] *End AF 1*


## *AF 2*

PG/AC = I Embrace/I Invite
QA = Challengingly
BP = The Plea
OB = Same
AM = Same
OS = Same
CX = Major
ST = Same


[Now this extremity
Hath brought me to thy hearth; not out of hope—
Mistake me not—to save my life, for if
I had fear'd death, of all the men i' the world
I would have 'voided thee, **QA (Piss-off-ed-ly)** but in mere spite,
To be full quit of those my banishers,
Stand I before thee here. **QA (Motivatingly)** Then if thou hast
A heart of wreak in thee, that wilt revenge
Thine own particular wrongs and stop those maims
Of shame seen through thy country, speed thee straight,
And make my misery serve thy turn: so use it

100 THE TRAGEDIES – WOMEN

That my revengeful services may prove
As benefits to thee, for I will fight
Against my canker'd country with the spleen
Of all the under fiends. **QA (Cards-on-the-table-ed-ly)** But if so be
Thou darest not this and that to prove more fortunes
Thou'rt tired, then, in a word, I also am
Longer to live most weary, and present
My throat to thee and to thy ancient malice;
Which not to cut would show thee but a fool,
Since I have ever follow'd thee with hate,
Drawn tuns of blood out of thy country's breast,
And cannot live but to thy shame, unless
It be to do thee service.] *End AF 2*

**Note: To do this speech well be sure to fight the atmosphere within—
Fear. Once again it is the struggle that we are most interested in.
Coriolanus is playing his final card in a den of lions. We must feel the
atmosphere and take joy in the fight.**

# Three

*Hamlet*
Act I, sc. iii

Polonius—AR—Father, Child Eternal, Politician, Teacher, Networker

## MONOLOGUE

### *AF 1*

PG/AC = I Push/I Urge
QA = Urgently
BP = The Short Goodbye
OB = I want Laertes to be on time.
AM = Mad
OS = The boat is about to sail.
CX = Auxiliary
ST = Laertes may miss the boat and not be at university on time.

# THE TRAGEDIES – WOMEN    101

**AR (Father)** [Yet here, Laertes! Aboard, aboard, for shame!
The wind sits in the shoulder of your sail,
And you are stay'd for. There, my blessing with thee!] *End AF 1*


## *AF 2*

PG/AC = I Embrace/I Instruct
QA = Importantly
BP = The Advice
OB = Same
AM = Fear
OS = Same
CX = Major
ST = Same


**AR (Teacher)** [And these few precepts in thy memory
See thou character. **QA (Firmly)** Give thy thoughts no tongue,
Nor any unproportioned thought his act.
**QA (Gently)** Be thou familiar, **QA (Sternly)** but by no means vulgar.
**QA (Fervently)** Those friends thou hast, and their adoption tried,
Grapple them to thy soul with hoops of steel;
**QA (Easily)** But do not dull thy palm with entertainment
Of each new-hatch'd, unfledged comrade. **QA (Cautiously)** Beware
Of entrance to a quarrel, **QA (Manly)** but being in,
Bear't that the opposed may beware of thee.
**QA (Importantly)** Give every man thy ear, **QA (Cautiously)** but few
   thy voice;
**QA (Importantly)** Take each man's censure, **QA (Cautiously)** but
   reserve thy judgment.
**QA (Oh-my-Godly)** Neither a borrower nor a lender be;
For loan oft loses both itself and friend,
And borrowing dulls the edge of husbandry.
**QA (Most-important-of-all-ly)** This above all: to thine ownself be
   true,
And it must follow, as the night the day,
Thou canst not then be false to any man.
**AR (Father) QA (Dotingly)** Farewell: my blessing season this in
   thee!] *End AF 2*

102              THE TRAGEDIES – WOMEN

**Note: The fun in this speech is the quick changes in QA's. The ship is about to sail and Polonius is anxious for his son to board—but not without some wise advice.**

# Four

*Julius Caesar*
Act I, sc. ii

Cassius—AR—Politician, Child Devine, Poet, Warrior

## MONOLOGUE

### *AF 1*

PG/AC = I Embrace/I Butter-Up
QA = Admiringly
BP = The Weak Demi-God
OB = I want Brutus on my side.
AM = Mad
OS = Brutus is not yet completely swayed.
CX = Major (building)
ST = If Caesar finds out I am plotting he will kill me.


**AR (Politician)** [I know that virtue to be in you, Brutus,
As well as I do know your outward favour.
**QA (Sum-up-ed-ly)** Well, honour is the subject of my story.
**PG (I Lift/I Compare) QA (Matter-of-fact-ly)** I cannot tell what
     you and other men
Think of this life; but, for my single self,
**QA (Proudly)** I had as lief not be as live to be
In awe of such a thing as I myself.
**QA (Levelly)** I was born free as Caesar; so were you.
We both have fed as well, and we can both
Endure the winter's cold as well as he.
**PG (I Open) QA (Reportedly)** For once, upon a raw and gusty day,
The troubled Tiber chafing with her shores,
Caesar said to me **QA (Condescendingly)** 'Darest thou, Cassius,
     now

## THE TRAGEDIES – WOMEN

Leap in with me into this angry flood,
And swim to yonder point?' **QA (Daringly)** Upon the word,
Accoutred as I was, I plunged in
And bade him follow; **QA (Baitingly)** so indeed he did.
**QA (Manly)** The torrent roar'd, and we did buffet it
With lusty sinews, throwing it aside
And stemming it with hearts of controversy.
**QA (Frightfully)** But ere we could arrive the point proposed,
Caesar cried 'Help me, Cassius, or I sink!'
**PG (I Lift) QA (Proudly)** I, as Aeneas, our great ancestor,
Did from the flames of Troy upon his shoulder
The old Anchises bear, so from the waves of Tiber
Did I the tired Caesar. **PG (I Close) QA (Dejectedly)** And this man
Is now become a god, and Cassius is
A wretched creature and must bend his body,
If Caesar carelessly but nod on him.
**PG (I Open/I Reveal) QA (Fearfully)** He had a fever when he was
   in Spain,
And when the fit was on him, I did mark
How he did shake: 'tis true, this god did shake;
His coward lips did from their colour fly,
And that same eye whose bend doth awe the world
Did lose his lustre. **QA (Mockingly)** I did hear him groan;
Ay, and that tongue of his that bade the Romans
Mark him and write his speeches in their books,
Alas, it cried 'Give me some drink, Titinius,'
**QA (Disgustingly)** As a sick girl. **PG (I Penetrate/I Bait) QA (Unbe-
   lievably)** Ye gods, it doth
amaze me
A man of such a feeble temper should
So get the start of the majestic world
And bear the palm alone.] *End AF 1*


**Note: Cassius must be careful in attempting to win over Brutus. The atmosphere of Fear is strong, and Cassius should work to overcome that Fear. Yet, we still must feel it. Exercise on Radiation and you will come to know how to experience the subjective atmosphere so the audience senses it and how, as the character, to overcome it.**

# 104 THE TRAGEDIES – WOMEN

## Five

*Julius Caesar*
Act II, sc. i

Brutus—AR—Politician, Child Divine, Scholar, Tyrant

## MONOLOGUE

### *AF 1*

PG/AC = I Push/I Warn
QA = Firmly
BP = The Best Path
OB = I want for us to choose the best path.
AM = Fear
OS = Everyone must be on the same page.
CX = Major (building)
ST = If anything should go wrong we will all be dead.

**AR (Politician)** [Our course will seem too bloody, Caius
   Cassius,
To cut the head off and then hack the limbs,
Like wrath in death and envy afterwards;
For Antony is but a limb of Caesar.
**PG (I Embrace) QA (Reasonably)** Let us be sacrificers, **QA (Uneas-
   ily)** but not butchers,
Caius.
**QA (Unitingly)** We all stand up against the spirit of Caesar;
And in the spirit of men there is no blood.
**QA (Wishingly)** O, that we then could come by Caesar's spirit,
And not dismember Caesar! **QA (Dejectedly)** But, alas,
Caesar must bleed for it. And, gentle friends,
**QA (Boldly)** Let's kill him boldly, **QA (Warningly)** but not wrath-
   fully;
**QA (Befittingly)** Let's carve him as a dish fit for the gods,
**QA (Unbefittingly)** Not hew him as a carcass fit for hounds.
**QA (Cunningly)** And let our hearts, as subtle masters do,
Stir up their servants to an act of rage,

# THE TRAGEDIES – WOMEN    105

And after seem to chide 'em. **QA (Cover-our-ass-ed-ly)** This shall make
Our purpose necessary and not envious:
Which so appearing to the common eyes,
We shall be call'd purgers, not murderers.
**QA (Unthreateningly)** And for Mark Antony, think not of him;
For he can do no more than Caesar's arm
When Caesar's head is off.] *End AF 1*


**Note: Brutus is a cool and cruel customer. You must decide if his Actions are noble or selfish. You may be able to discern my personal choice by my AC's and QA's.**


## Six

*Julius Caesar*
Act III, sc. i


Antony—AR—Warrior, Child Divine, Lover, Olympian

## SOLILOQUY

### *AF 1*

PG/AC = I Embrace/I Beg
QA = Pleadingly
BP = The Apology
OB = I want to honor Caesar.
AM = Mad
OS = Finding his murderers.
CX = Auxiliary
ST = The survival of Rome!


**AR (Olympian)** [O, pardon me, thou bleeding piece of earth,
That I am meek and gentle with these butchers!
Thou art the ruins of the noblest man
That ever lived in the tide of times.
**AR (Warrior) QA (Threateningly)** Woe to the hand that shed this costly blood!] *End AF 1*

# 106    THE TRAGEDIES – WOMEN

## *AF 2*

PG/AC = I Wring/I Promise
QA = Faithfully
BP = The Vow
OB = I want vengeance!
AM = Same
OS = Same
CX = Major
ST = Same


[Over thy wounds now do I prophesy,
Which, like dumb mouths, do ope their ruby lips,
To beg the voice and utterance of my tongue—
**PG (I Smash) QA (Assuredly)** A curse shall light upon the limbs
    of men;
Domestic fury and fierce civil strife
Shall cumber all the parts of Italy;
Blood and destruction shall be so in use
And dreadful objects so familiar
That mothers shall but smile when they behold
Their infants quarter'd with the hands of war,
All pity choked with custom of fell deeds;
**PG (I Open) QA (Triumphantly)** And Caesar's spirit, ranging for
    revenge,
With Ate by his side come hot from hell,
Shall in these confines with a monarch's voice
Cry 'Havoc,' and let slip the dogs of war,
That this foul deed shall smell above the earth
With carrion men, groaning for burial.] *End AF 2*


**Note: Antony is mad indeed. Be careful not to fall into the trap of playing the emotion. This soliloquy is too often done by screaming it from the beginning. Along with being mad, Antony is also sad to have lost his father figure to an end such as this. Yes, the objective atmosphere is Mad. Find the nuances of Sad within the speech, and you'll find varied tempos and rhythms. Remember to build a dynamic RW.**

# THE TRAGEDIES – WOMEN      107

## Seven

*King Lear*
Act I, sc. ii

Edmund—AR—Lover, Child Orphan, Victim, Dreamer, Mystic

## SOLILOQUY

### *AF 1*

PG/AC = I Open/I Pledge
QA = Wholeheartedly
BP = The Pledge
OB = I want the aid of nature.
AM = Fear
OS = There is no answer—only my faith in nature.
CX = Auxiliary
ST = My entire future depends on my immediate Actions.


**AR (Dreamer)** [Thou, nature, art my goddess; to thy law
My services are bound.] *End AF 1*


### *AF 2*

PG/AC = I Pull/I Invite
QA = Reasonably
BP = The Turn (to turn the audience's support to me)
OB = I want everyone to see my side and support me.
AM = Glad
OS = Same
CX = Major
ST = Same


**AR (Victim)** [Wherefore should I
Stand in the plague of custom, and permit
The curiosity of nations to deprive me,
For that I am some twelve or fourteen moon-shines

Lag of a brother? Why bastard? **QA (Demeaningly)** Wherefore base?

**QA (Charmingly)** When my dimensions are as well compact,
My mind as generous, and my shape as true,
As honest madam's issue? **QA (Lovingly—to audience)** Why brand they us
With base? **QA (Sadly)** with baseness? **QA (Unbelievably)** bastardy? **QA (Angrily)** base, base?
**PG (I Embrace) QA (Challengingly)** Who, in the lusty stealth of nature, take
More composition and fierce quality
Than doth, within a dull, stale, tired bed,
Go to the creating a whole tribe of fops,
Got 'tween asleep and wake? **PG (I Smash) QA (That's-it-ly)** Well, then,
Legitimate Edgar, I must have your land.
**PG (I Close) QA (Angrily)** Our father's love is to the bastard Edmund
As to the legitimate. Fine word, legitimate!
**PG (I Open) QA (Hopefully)** Well, my legitimate, if this letter speed,
And my invention thrive, Edmund the base
Shall top the legitimate. I grow; I prosper:
**QA (Pleadingly)** Now, gods, stand up for bastards!] *End AF 1*

**Note: This speech of Edmund's is very often done for auditions. It is a perfect length and is delicious for the actor to chew on. The problem is that most actors see it mostly as an angry rant against Gloucester and the law concerning bastardy. It's not only that at all.**

**The actor should take into account that this is a soliloquy and is meant to be addressed directly to the audience. You have one chance in the entire play to get the audience to see your point of view and this is it. If you can get the audience to like you the villainy will be that much more delightful. So—get the audience on your side via your charming personality, good looks, and reason. Were I doing this speech I'd imagine I was addressing an audience filled with bastards—just like me! Chekhov suggested we see the objective completed before we begin our Actions. This is great advice. We have succeeded before we have begun.**

# THE TRAGEDIES – WOMEN     109

## Eight

*Macbeth*
Act I, sc. vii

Macbeth—AR—King, Child Divine, Lover, Warrior, Olympian, Diplomat

## SOLILOQUY

### *AF 1*

PG/AC = I Penetrate/I Solve (the puzzle)
QA = Wishfully
BP = The Crux
OB = I want to come to a conclusion.
AM = Fear
OS = Duncan is a good King. The conflict in myself.
CX = Major (building)
ST = The ultimate rule of the realm!

**AR (Diplomat)** [If it were done when 'tis done, then 'twere well
It were done quickly: if the assassination
Could trammel up the consequence, and catch
With his surcease success; that but this blow
Might be the be-all and the end-all here,
**QA (Back-to-earth-ly)** But here, upon this bank and shoal of time,
We'd jump the life to come. But in these cases
We still have judgment here; that we but teach
Bloody instructions, which, being taught, return
To plague the inventor: **QA (Realistically)** this even-handed justice
Commends the ingredients of our poison'd chalice
To our own lips. **QA (Reasonably—to reason it out)** He's here in
    double trust;
First, as I am his kinsman and his subject,
Strong both against the deed; then, as his host,
**(Chidingly—to self)** Who should against his murderer shut the
    door,
Not bear the knife myself. **QA (Admiringly)** Besides, this Duncan
Hath borne his faculties so meek, hath been

110     THE TRAGEDIES – WOMEN

So clear in his great office, that his virtues
Will plead like angels, trumpet-tongued, against
The deep damnation of his taking-off;
And pity, like a naked new-born babe,
Striding the blast, or heaven's cherubim, horsed
Upon the sightless couriers of the air,
Shall blow the horrid deed in every eye,
That tears shall drown the wind. **QA (Concludingly)** I have no spur
To prick the sides of my intent, but only
Vaulting ambition, which o'erleaps itself
And falls on the other.] *End AF 1*

**Note: Look at the next to last QA—Admiringly. When you have a long period of time before a QA change you must build carefully and use tempo.**

# Nine

*Othello*
Act I, sc. i

Iago—AR—Politician, Child Orphan, Rebel, Networker, Gambler,
    Victim, Warrior

## MONOLOGUE

### *AF 1*

PG/AC = I Embrace/I Seduce
QA = Reassuringly
BP = The Offense
OB = I want Roderigo's 'help' (he dupes Roderigo) for revenge
    upon Othello.
AM = Mad
OS = I need more people on my side.
CX = Major
ST = There is a lot of 'networking' (manipulating) to do.

**AR (Gambler)** [O, sir, content you;
I follow him to serve my turn upon him.

THE TRAGEDIES – WOMEN 111

We cannot all be masters, nor all masters
Cannot be truly follow'd. **QA (Condescendingly)** You shall mark
Many a duteous and knee-crooking knave,
That, doting on his own obsequious bondage,
Wears out his time, much like his master's ass,
For nought but provender, and when he's old, cashier'd.
**QA (Declaringly)** Whip me such honest knaves. **QA (Secretly)** Others there are
Who, trimm'd in forms and visages of duty,
Keep yet their hearts attending on themselves,
And, throwing but shows of service on their lords,
Do well thrive by them and when they have lined their coats
Do themselves homage: these fellows have some soul;
**QA (Proudly)** And such a one do I profess myself. **QA (Profoundly)** For, sir,
It is as sure as you are Roderigo,
Were I the Moor, I would not be Iago.
**QA (Swearingly)** In following him, I follow but myself;
Heaven is my judge, not I for love and duty,
But seeming so, for my peculiar end:
**PG (I Smash) QA (Promisingly)** For when my outward Action doth demonstrate
The native act and figure of my heart
In compliment extern, 'tis not long after
But I will wear my heart upon my sleeve
For daws to peck at: **QA (Greedily)** I am not what I am.] *End AF 1*

**Note: What a fun monologue. Iago is angry in being passed over for promotion. Yet, he must control his anger to get what he wants. It is a great example of Chekhov's 'inner-outer' tempo.**

## Ten

*Romeo and Juliet*
Act II, sc. ii

Romeo—AR—Lover, Child Eternal, Prince, Rebel, Poet

# MONOLOGUE

## *AF 1*

PG/AC = I Embrace/I Worship

QA = Giddily

BP = The Overture

OB = I want to find the exact words to describe my love!

AM = Glad

OS = Her parents may discover me.

CX = Major (building)

ST = If I am caught her parents will find a way for us to never see each other again.


**AR (Lover)** [But, soft! What light through yonder window breaks?

It is the east, and Juliet is the sun.

Arise, fair sun, and kill the envious moon,

Who is already sick and pale with grief,

That thou her maid art far more fair than she.

**QA (Chidingly)** Be not her maid, since she is envious;

Her vestal livery is but sick and green

And none but fools do wear it; cast it off.

**QA (Adoringly)** It is my lady, O, it is my love!

**QA (Wishfully)** O, that she knew she were!

**QA (Quizzically)** She speaks yet she says nothing: what of that?

Her eye discourses; I will answer it.

**PG (I Close) QA (Disappointingly)** I am too bold, 'tis not to me she speaks.

**PG (I Embrace) QA (Lovingly)** Two of the fairest stars in all the heaven,

Having some business, do entreat her eyes

To twinkle in their spheres till they return.

**PG (I Open) QA (Comparatively)** What if her eyes were there, they in her head?

The brightness of her cheek would shame those stars,

As daylight doth a lamp; her eyes in heaven

Would through the airy region stream so bright

# THE TRAGEDIES – WOMEN 113

That birds would sing and think it were not night.

**PG (I Embrace) QA (Adoringly)** See, how she leans her cheek
upon her hand!

O, that I were a glove upon that hand,

That I might touch that cheek!

**QA (Faintingly)** She speaks!

O, speak again, bright angel! For thou art

As glorious to this night, being o'er my head

As is a winged messenger of heaven

Unto the white-upturned wondering eyes

Of mortals that fall back to gaze on him

When he bestrides the lazy-pacing clouds

And sails upon the bosom of the air.] *End AF 1*

**Note: Romeo's subjective AM (Glad) more specifically shifts between
Romance and Lust. It may seem a fine line yet it is important for the PL
in the speech. Find the shifts in the AM's in the QA's.**

## Eleven

*Titus Andronicus*
Act III, sc. ii

Titus—AR—Warrior, Child Wounded, Avenger, Father, Victim

### MONOLOGUE

### *AF 1*

PG/AC = I Wring/I Chide

QA = Admonishingly

BP = The Hard Truth (Woe is Me)

OB = I want all the cards on the table . . . to advise Lavinia not to
suffer anymore.

AM = Mad

OS = Marcus thinks I am insane and is fighting me.

CX = Major

ST = Could circumstances be any worse?

# 114 THE TRAGEDIES – WOMEN

**AR (Victim)** [How now! Has sorrow made thee dote already?
Why, Marcus, no man should be mad but I.
What violent hands can she lay on her life?
Ah, wherefore dost thou urge the name of hands;
To bid Aeneas tell the tale twice o'er,
How Troy was burnt and he made miserable?
**PG (I Close) QA (Mournfully)** O, handle not the theme, to talk of hands,
Lest we remember still that we have none.
**PG (I Push) QA (Angrily)** Fie, fie, how franticly I square my talk,
As if we should forget we had no hands,
If Marcus did not name the word of hands!
**PG (I Embrace) QA (Gently)** Come, let's fall to; and, gentle girl, eat this.
**PG (I Push) QA (Excitedly)** Here is no drink! Hark, Marcus, what she says;
I can interpret all her martyr'd signs;
**QA (Sorrowfully)** She says she drinks no other drink but tears,
Brew'd with her sorrow, mesh'd upon her cheeks.
**PG (I Embrace) QA (Comfortingly)** Speechless complainer, I will learn thy thought;
In thy dumb Action will I be as perfect
As begging hermits in their holy prayers:
**QA (Protectively)** Thou shalt not sigh, nor hold thy stumps to heaven,
Nor wink, nor nod, nor kneel, nor make a sign,
But I of these will wrest an alphabet
And by still practise learn to know thy meaning.] *End AF 1*

**Note: Is Titus mad (insane) or not? The circumstances he and his family have been through could certainly drive anyone mad. In the end it really doesn't matter as the actor cannot play madness. Remember we can only play AC's and QA's. With that said could madness guide your choices? You have to make some decisions in this one. Don't make those decisions with your 'dry intellect.' Instead, make those decisions on your feet and find your choices organically through the given circumstances.**

THE TRAGEDIES – WOMEN 115

# Twelve

*Titus Andronicus*
Act IV, sc. ii

Aaron— AR—Servant, Child Orphan, Lover, Father

## MONOLOGUE

### *AF 1*

PG/AC = I Tear/I Threaten
QA = Furiously
BP = The Killers
OB = I want to protect my son!
AM = Mad
OS = I am outnumbered.
CX = Major
ST = The life of my son!


**AR (Father)** [Stay, murderous villains! Will you kill your brother?
Now, by the burning tapers of the sky,
That shone so brightly when this boy was got,
He dies upon my scimitar's sharp point
That touches this my first-born son and heir!
**QA (Protectively)** I tell you, younglings, not Enceladus,
With all his threatening band of Typhon's brood,
Nor great Alcides, nor the god of war,
Shall seize this prey out of his father's hands.
**QA (Provokingly)** What, what, ye sanguine, shallow-hearted boys!
Ye white-limed walls! Ye alehouse painted signs!
**QA (Caringly)** Coal-black is better than another hue,
In that it scorns to bear another hue;
For all the water in the ocean
Can never turn the swan's black legs to white,
Although she lave them hourly in the flood.
**PG (I Close) QA (Defiantly)**Tell the empress from me, I am of
    age
To keep mine own, excuse it how she can.] *End AF 1*

116 THE TRAGEDIES – WOMEN

**Note: This is yet another monologue where the actor could get into an angry rant from the beginning and push it through to the end. Don't. Especially invest in the next to last QA, Caringly (or whatever QA you find on your feet). The tempo should slow down here rather dramatically.**

### End Chapter Four

Other speeches to consider from the Tragedies (Index of First Lines)

1. *Antony and Cleopatra*
   Act V, sc. ii
   Cleopatra—'Sir, I will eat no meat. . . '

2. *Antony and Cleopatra*
   Act V, sc. ii
   Cleopatra—'No matter, sir, what I have heard or known. . . '

3. *Antony and Cleopatra*
   Act V, sc. ii
   Cleopatra—'Give me my robe. . . '

4. *Hamlet*
   Act I, sc. ii
   Hamlet—'O that this too too sullied flesh. . . '

5. *Hamlet*
   Act II, sc. ii
   Polonius—'My liege, and madam, to expostulate. . . '

6. *Hamlet*
   Act II, sc. ii
   Hamlet—'Now I am alone . . . O what a rogue and peasant slave. . . '

7. *Hamlet*
   Act III, sc. i
   Hamlet—'To be, or not to be. . . '

8. *Hamlet*
   Act III, sc. iii
   Hamlet—'Now I might do it pat. . . '

9. *Julius Caesar* (cut speech)
   Act II, sc. i

# THE TRAGEDIES – WOMEN                    117

Portia—'Y'have ungently, Brutus. . . ' through 'Make me acquainted with your cause of grief. . . '

10. *Julius Caesar* (cut speech)
Act II, sc. ii
Calphurnia—'What mean, you, Caesar. . . ' through 'The heavens themselves blaze forth the death of princes.'

11. *King Lear*
Act I, sc. ii
Edmund—'This is the excellent foppery of the world. . . '

12. *King Lear*
Act II, sc. iv
King Lear—'O reason not the need. . . '

13. *Macbeth*
Act II, sc. i
Macbeth—'Is this a dagger. . . '

14. *Macbeth*
Act II, sc. iii
Porter—'Here's a knocking, indeed. . . '

15. *Othello*
Act I, sc. iii
Othello—'Her father loved me. . . '

16. *Othello*
Act I, sc. iii
Iago—'Thus do I ever make my fool my purse. . . '

17. *Romeo and Juliet*
Act I, sc. iv
Mercutio—'O then I see Queen Mab hath been with you. . . '

18. *Romeo and Juliet*
Act II, sc. ii
Juliet—'O Romeo, Romeo, wherefore art thou Romeo. . . '

19. *Romeo and Juliet*
Act II, sc. ii
Juliet—'Thou knowest the mask of night is on my face. . . '

20. *Romeo and Juliet*
Act II, sc. v
Juliet—'The clock struck nine when I did send the Nurse. . . '

# THE TRAGEDIES – WOMEN

21. *Romeo and Juliet*
    Act III, sc. ii
    Juliet—'Shall I speak of him that is my husband. . . '

22. *Romeo and Juliet*
    Act III, sc. iii
    Romeo—'Tis torture and not mercy. . . '

23. *Timon of Athens*
    Act IV, sc. iii
    Timon—'Thou art a slave, whom Fortune's tender arm. . . '

# Chapter Five

# THE HISTORIES – WOMEN

## One

*Richard II*
Act I, sc. ii

Duchess of Gloucester—AR—Princess, Child Divine, Avenger, Victim

### MONOLOGUE

### *AF 1*

PG/AC = I Penetrate/I Challenge
QA = Throw-Down-the-Gauntlet-ly
BP = The Rightful Vengeance
OB = I want revenge for my husband's murder.
AM = Mad
OS = Gaunt may refuse for political reasons.
CX = Major (building)
ST = Where will the murders end unless we stop the murderer?

**AR (Avenger)** [Finds brotherhood in thee no sharper spur?
Hath love in thy old blood no living fire?
**PG (I Open) QA (Reasonably)** Edward's seven sons, whereof thy-
self art one,
Were as seven vials of his sacred blood,
Or seven fair branches springing from one root:

120 THE HISTORIES – WOMEN

Some of those seven are dried by nature's course,
Some of those branches by the Destinies cut;
**PG (I Wring) QA (Angrily)** But Thomas, my dear lord, my life, my
Gloucester,
One vial full of Edward's sacred blood,
One flourishing branch of his most royal root,
Is crack'd, and all the precious liquor spilt,
Is hack'd down, and his summer leaves all faded,
By envy's hand and murder's bloody axe.
**PG (I Embrace) QA (Beggingly)** Ah, Gaunt, his blood was thine!
**QA (Comparatively)** That
bed, that womb,
That metal, that self-mould, that fashion'd thee
Made him a man; and though thou livest and breathest,
Yet art thou slain in him: thou dost consent
In some large measure to thy father's death,
In that thou seest thy wretched brother die,
Who was the model of thy father's life.
**PG (I Open) QA (Despairingly)** Call it not patience, Gaunt; it is
despair:
In suffering thus thy brother to be slaughter'd,
Thou showest the naked pathway to thy life,
Teaching stern murder how to butcher thee.
That which in mean men we intitle patience
Is pale cold cowardice in noble breasts.
**QA (Conclusively)** What shall I say? To safeguard thine own
life,
The best way is to venge my Gloucester's death.] *End AF 1*


**Note: There are some longer passages here between QA's. Be sure to
build these in intensity. Think of it this way . . . the intensity builds from
1–4 on a scale of 1–5. The only reason you don't reach 5 is that it would
then be purging emotion. It is far more interesting to see the character
take hold of herself just before she loses it completely than to see her
purging. If the character purges the audience deflates. In Chekhov we
call this 'expansion and contraction.' Don't allow the character to ever
completely purge. Instead, at the near height of expansion—contract
instead by changing QA's.**

# THE HISTORIES – WOMEN

## Two

*Henry IV, Part Two*
Act II, sc. iii

Lady Percy—AR—Princess, Child Divine, Healer, Victim

## MONOLOGUE

### *AF 1*

PG/AC = I Push/I Demand
QA = Aggressively
BP = The Clearer Path
OB = I want Henry to stand down.
AM = Mad/Sad
OS = Henry is bent for war and wants to keep his promise.
CX = Major (building)
ST = More death.


**AR (Victim)** [O yet, for God's sake, go not to these wars!
**PG (I Embrace) QA (Reasonably)** The time was, father, that you
    broke your word,
When you were more endeared to it than now;
**QA (Pridefully-his own)** When your own Percy, **QA (Lovingly)**
    when my heart's dear Harry,
**QA (Accusingly)** Threw many a northward look to see his father
Bring up his powers; but he did long in vain.
Who then persuaded you to stay at home?
There were two honours lost, yours and your son's.
**QA (Pleadingly)** For yours, the God of heaven brighten it!
**QA (Pridefully-her own)** For his, it stuck upon him as the sun
In the grey vault of heaven, and by his light
Did all the chivalry of England move
To do brave acts: **QA (Adoringly)** he was indeed the glass
Wherein the noble youth did dress themselves:
**QA (Plainly)** He had no legs that practised not his gait;
**QA (Wonderingly)** And speaking thick, which nature made his
    blemish,

122                THE HISTORIES – WOMEN

Became the accents of the valiant;
**QA (Truthfully)** For those that could speak low and tardily
Would turn their own perfection to abuse,
To seem like him: **QA (Wonderingly)** so that in speech, **QA (Plainly)**
    in gait,
**QA (Everythingly)** In diet, in affections of delight,
In military rules, humours of blood,
**QA (Wonderingly)** He was the mark and glass, copy and book,
That fashion'd others. And him, **QA (Celebratedly)** O wondrous him!
O miracle of men! **QA (I Wring) QA (Accusingly)** Him did you leave,
Second to none, unseconded by you,
To look upon the hideous god of war
In disadvantage; to abide a field
Where nothing but the sound of Hotspur's name
Did seem defensible: **QA (Cards-on-the-table-ly)** so you left him.
**PG (I Embrace/I Beg) QA (Pleadingly)** Never, O never, do his
    ghost the wrong
To hold your honour more precise and nice
With others than with him! **QA (Demandingly)** Let them alone.
**QA (All-End-ly as in the poker term, the last straw)** The marshal
    and the archbishop are
strong:
Had my sweet Harry had but half their numbers,
To-day might I, hanging on Hotspur's neck,
Have talk'd of Monmouth's grave.] *End AF 1*

**Note: I didn't cut this monologue for length because it is just too
important for a student to work on the entire piece. I suppose I could
say that about many speeches in this book. If you use this speech for an
audition it will have to be cut. As always build the speech carefully and
pay careful attention to tempo. QA's often dictate tempo.**

## Three

*Henry V*
Prologue

Chorus—AR—Storyteller

# THE HISTORIES – WOMEN

## SOLILOQUY

### *AF 1*

PG/AC = I Open/I Invite
QA = Excitedly
BP = The Pumping Up
OB = I want the audience to turn-on their imaginations.
AM = Glad
OS = I must convince 300 people.
CX = Major (building)
ST = There are numerous challenges to imagine and the play must
 celebrate Henry's life. The Queen is in attendance.


**AR (Storyteller)** [O for a Muse of fire, that would ascend
The brightest heaven of invention,
A kingdom for a stage, princes to act
And monarchs to behold the swelling scene!
**QA (Warlikely)** Then should the warlike Harry, like himself,
Assume the port of Mars; and at his heels,
Leash'd in like hounds, should famine, sword and fire
Crouch for employment. **PG (I Embrace) QA (Gently)** But par-
 don, and gentles all,
The flat unraised spirits that have dared
On this unworthy scaffold to bring forth
So great an object: **QA (Challengingly)** can this cockpit hold
The vasty fields of France? O may we cram
Within this wooden O the very casques
That did affright the air at Agincourt?
**QA (Beggingly)** O, pardon! Since a crooked figure may
Attest in little place a million;
And let us, ciphers to this great accompt,
On your imaginary forces work.
**QA (Teasingly)** Suppose within the girdle of these walls
Are now confined two mighty monarchies,
Whose high upreared and abutting fronts
The perilous narrow ocean parts asunder.
**QA (Easily)** Piece out our imperfections with your thoughts;
Into a thousand parts divide on man,

# 124 THE HISTORIES – WOMEN

And make imaginary puissance;
**QA (Heatedly—build please to next QA)** Think when we talk of
   horses, that you see them
Printing their proud hoofs i' the receiving earth;
For 'tis your thoughts that now must deck our kings,
Carry them here and there; jumping o'er times,
Turning the accomplishment of many years
Into an hour-glass! **QA (Gently)** For the which supply,
Admit me Chorus to this history;
Who prologue-like your humble patience pray,
Gently to hear, **QA (Kindly)** kindly to judge, our play.] *End AF 1*

**Note: You can always, while rehearsing, reinvest in your PG. In fact,
it is a good idea while finding, on your feet, how to build the speech
in volume, tempo, etc. Reinvestment in the PG also increases the will
power—making your radiation stronger. Reinvestment means to redo
the action from a place of readiness.**

## Four

*Henry VI, Pt. 1*
Act I, sc. ii

Joan de Pucelle—AR—Warrior, Child Divine, Savior

## MONOLOGUE

### *AF 1*

PG/AC = I Open/I Introduce
QA = Simply
BP = The Survival
OB = I want the Dauphin to allow me to lead troops into battle.
AM = Fear
OS = Will the Dauphin allow a woman to battle for France?
CX = Major (building)
ST = The survival of France.

**AR (Savior)** [Dauphin, I am by birth a shepherd's daughter,
My wit untrain'd in any kind of art.
Heaven and our Lady gracious hath it pleased

# THE HISTORIES – WOMEN 125

To shine on my contemptible estate.
**QA (Humbly)** Lo, whilst I waited on my tender lambs,
And to sun's parching heat display'd my cheeks,
God's mother deigned to appear to me
And in a vision full of majesty
Will'd me to leave my base vocation
And free my country from calamity.
**QA (Glorify-ing-ly)** Her aid she promised and assured success:
In complete glory she reveal'd herself;
And, whereas I was black and swart before,
With those clear rays which she infused on me
That beauty am I bless'd with which you see.
**QA (Challengingly)** Ask me what question thou canst possible,
And I will answer unpremeditated:
**QA (Daringly)** My courage try by combat, if thou darest,
And thou shalt find that I exceed my sex.
Resolve on this, thou shalt be fortunate,
If thou receive me for thy warlike mate.] *End AF 1*

**Note: This brief speech is very powerful when paired with a character
such as Phoebe from *As You Like It*. Bring the stakes into a modern
context. It is unheard of for a woman to lead troops into battle. Joan
must convince the Dauphin that she has indeed been given this course
by the Virgin Mary. You have to fantasize the visitation of the Holy
Mother to Joan to make this speech work.**

## Five

*Henry VI, Pt. II*
Act I, sc. iii

Queen Margaret—Queen, Divine Child, Prostitute

## MONOLOGUE

### *AF 1*

PG/AC = I Throw (out this question)/I Propose
QA = Puzzledly
BP = The Conundrum

126 THE HISTORIES – WOMEN

OB = I want Suffolk to help me solve the problem.
AM = Mad
OS = The King is less than kingly.
CX = Major (building)
ST = I may have to live my entire life in despair.

**AR (Queen)** [My Lord of Suffolk, say, is this the guise,
Is this the fashion in the court of England?
Is this the government of Britain's isle,
And this the royalty of Albion's king?
**QA (Bitchily)** What shall King Henry be a pupil still
Under the surly Gloucester's governance?
Am I a queen in title and in style,
And must be made a subject to a duke?
**QA (Proudly)** I tell thee, Pole, when in the city Tours
Thou ran'st a tilt in honour of my love
And stolest away the ladies' hearts of France,
**QA (Disappointedly)** I thought King Henry had resembled thee
In courage, courtship and proportion.
But all his mind is bent to holiness,
To number Ave-Maries on his beads;
**QA (Hatefully)** His champions are the prophets and apostles,
His weapons holy saws of sacred writ,
His study is his tilt-yard, and his loves
Are brazen images of canonized saints.
**QA (Sarcastically)** I would the college of the cardinals
Would choose him pope, and carry him to Rome,
And set the triple crown upon his head:
That were a state fit for 'his holiness.'] *End AF 1*

**Note: Just be aware that whatever QA's you find you should search for
Polarity. Otherwise this speech could be a 'one-trick-pony.'**

## Six

*Henry Six, Pt. II*
Act II, sc. iv

Eleanor—AR—Princess, Child Nature, Rebel, Witch

# MONOLOGUE

## *AF 1*

PG/AC = I Push/I Warn
QA = Accusingly
BP = The Vow
OB = I want Humphrey to know my shame and be warned.
AM = Mad
OS = I am banished. It will be a difficult path to vengeance.
CX = Major (Building)
ST = To live through this walk of shame.


**AR (Rebel)** [Come you, my lord, to see my open shame?
Now thou dost penance too. Look how they gaze!
See how the giddy multitude do point,
And nod their heads, and throw their eyes on thee!
**QA (Pleadingly)** Ah, Gloucester, hide thee from their hateful looks,
And, in thy closet pent up, rue my shame,
And ban thine enemies, both mine and thine!
Ah, Gloucester, teach me to forget myself!
**QA (Shamefully)** For whilst I think I am thy married wife
And thou a prince, protector of this land,
Methinks I should not thus be led along,
Mail'd up in shame, with papers on my back,
And followed with a rabble that rejoice
To see my tears and hear my deep-fet groans.
**QA (Hurtfully)** The ruthless flint doth cut my tender feet,
And when I start, the envious people laugh
And bid me be advised how I tread.
**QA (Tearfully)** Ah, Humphrey, can I bear this shameful yoke?
Trow'st thou that e'er I'll look upon the world,
Or count them happy that enjoy the sun?
**QA (Resolvedly)** No; dark shall be my light and night my day;
To think upon my pomp shall be my hell.
**QA (Promisingly)** Sometime I'll say, I am Duke Humphrey's wife,
And he a prince and ruler of the land:
Yet so he ruled and such a prince he was
As he stood by whilst I, his forlorn duchess,
Was made a wonder and a pointing-stock

128 THE HISTORIES – WOMEN

To every idle rascal follower.
**QA (Coolly)** But be thou mild and blush not at my shame,
Nor stir at nothing till the axe of death
Hang over thee, **QA (Assuredly)** as, sure, it shortly will.] *End AF 1*

**Note: Are you beginning to see a pattern in the women in the Histories? If you need a strong women's speech look no further than these plays.**

## Seven

*Henry VI, Pt. III*
Act I, sc. iv

Margaret—Queen, Divine Child, Victim, Avenger

## MONOLOGUE

### *AF 1*

PG/AC = I Penetrate/I Avenge
QA = Joyfully
BP = The Sweet Revenge
OB = I want vengeance.
AM = Glad
OS = Time. I want more to enjoy the moment.
CX = Major (building)
ST = What will the ruling family do? This is potentially dangerous
     business.

**AR (Avenger)** [Brave warriors, Clifford and Northumberland,
Come, make him stand upon this molehill here,
That raught at mountains with outstretched arms,
Yet parted but the shadow with his hand.
**QA (Gloatingly)** What! Was it you that would be England's king?
Was't you that revell'd in our parliament,
And made a preachment of your high descent?
Where are your mess of sons to back you now?

# THE HISTORIES – WOMEN                    129

**QA (Wantonly)** The wanton Edward, and the **QA (lustily)** lusty
George?
**QA (Hatefully)** And where's that valiant crook-back prodigy,
Dicky your boy, that with his grumbling voice
Was wont to cheer his dad in mutinies?
**QA (Sarcastically)** Or, with the rest, where is your darling Rutland?
**QA (Gloatingly)** Look, York: I stain'd this napkin with the blood
That valiant Clifford, with his rapier's point,
Made issue from the bosom of the boy;
And if thine eyes can water for his death,
I give thee this to dry thy cheeks withal.
**QA (Sarcastically)** Alas poor York! **QA (Hatefully)** But that I hate
thee deadly,
**QA (Lamentably)** I should lament thy miserable state.
I prithee, grieve, to make me merry, York.
**QA (Mockingly)** What, hath thy fiery heart so parch'd thine entrails
That not a tear can fall for Rutland's death?
Why art thou patient, man? Thou shouldst be mad;
And I, to make thee mad, do mock thee thus.
**QA (Giddily)** Stamp, rave, and fret, that I may sing and dance.
Thou wouldst be fee'd, I see, to make me sport.
York cannot speak, unless he wear a crown.
A crown for York! And, lords, bow low to him:
Hold you his hands, whilst I do set it on.
*Putting a paper crown on his head*
**QA (Mockingly)** Ay, marry, sir, now looks he like a king!
Ay, this is he that took King Henry's chair,
And this is he was his adopted heir.
But how is it that great Plantagenet
Is crown'd so soon, and broke his solemn oath?
**QA (Calculatingly)** Off with the crown, and with the crown his
head;
And, whilst we breathe, take time to do him dead.] *End AF1*

---

**Note: There are some lines near the end that have been cut for audition
length. If the actor is working on this speech for class purposes and not
an audition, I'd suggest reinserting the cut lines. Otherwise, enjoy the
sweet vengeance Margaret experiences. Fantasize that feeling.**

# Eight

*Richard III*
Act I, sc. ii

Lady Anne—AR—Princess, Child Divine, Dreamer, Slave, Victim

## MONOLOGUE

### *AF 1*

PG/AC = I Open/I Honor
QA = Lamentably
BP = The Honored Father (in-law)
OB = I want all to know what an honorable man he was.
AM = Mad
OS = The houses are divided.
CX = Major (building)
ST = Richard is a murderer. Who will be next?


**AR (Victim)** Set down, set down your honourable load,
**QA (Bitterly)** If honour may be shrouded in a hearse,
**QA (Lamentably)** Whilst I awhile obsequiously lament
The untimely fall of virtuous Lancaster.
Poor key-cold figure of a holy king,
Pale ashes of the house of Lancaster,
Thou bloodless remnant of that royal blood,
**QA (Angrily)** Be it lawful that I invocate thy ghost,
To hear the lamentations of Poor Anne,
Wife to thy Edward, to thy slaughter'd son,
Stabb'd by the selfsame hand that made these wounds!
**PG (I Embrace) QA (Weepingly)** Lo, in these windows that let forth
    thy life,
I pour the helpless balm of my poor eyes.
Cursed be the hand that made these fatal holes!
**QA (Cursedly)** Cursed be the heart that had the heart to do it!
    **Note: Build carefully to next QA.**
Cursed the blood that let this blood from hence!
More direful hap betide that hated wretch,
That makes us wretched by the death of thee,

THE HISTORIES – WOMEN     131

Than I can wish to adders, spiders, toads,
Or any creeping venom'd thing that lives!
If ever he have child, abortive be it,
Prodigious, and untimely brought to light,
Whose ugly and unnatural aspect
May fright the hopeful mother at the view;
And that be heir to his unhappiness! **(Major Climax)**
**QA (Hopefully)** If ever he have wife, let her he made
A miserable by the death of him
As I am made by my poor lord and thee!
**QA (Respectfully)** Come, now towards Chertsey with your holy
    load,
Taken from Paul's to be interred there;
And still, as you are weary of the weight,
Rest you, whiles I lament King Henry's corse.] *End AF 1*

**Note: Careful that this speech does not become one that purges emotion. Remember that purging takes the audience out of the moment. When you purge they do as well.**

## APPLICATION OF THE MICHAEL CHEKHOV TECHNIQUE TO SHAKESPEARE'S MONOLOGUES AND SOLILOQUIES

### *THE HISTORIES-MEN*

### One

*Richard II*
Act II, sc. i

John of Gaunt—AR—Prince, Child Divine, Warrior, Prophet

### MONOLOGUE

### *AF 1*

PG/AC = I Open/I Predict
QA = Friendly
BP = The Facts

# 132 THE HISTORIES – WOMEN

OB = I want York to help save the realm.
AM = Sad
OS = Will York actually listen to reason?
CX = Auxiliary
ST = The ruination of England.


**AR (Prophet)** [Methinks I am a prophet new inspired
And thus expiring do foretell of him:
**QA (Rashly)** His rash fierce blaze of riot cannot last,
For violent fires soon burn out themselves;
**QA (Wisely)** Small showers last long, but sudden storms are short;
**QA (Warningly)** He tires betimes that spurs too fast betimes;
With eager feeding food doth choke the feeder;
Light vanity, insatiate cormorant,
Consuming means, soon preys upon itself.] *End AF 1*


## *AF 2*

PG/AC = I Lift/I Exalt
QA = Devotedly
BP = The Reason (to save the realm)
OB = Same
AM = Fear
OS = Same
CX = Major (building)
ST = Same


[This royal throne of kings, this scepter'd isle,
**QA (Majestically)** This earth of majesty, this seat of Mars,
This other Eden, demi-paradise,
**QA (Protectively)** This fortress built by Nature for herself
Against infection and the hand of war,
**QA (Happily)** This happy breed of men, this little world,
**QA (Lovingly)** This precious stone set in the silver sea,
**QA (Sternly)** Which serves it in the office of a wall,
Or as a moat defensive to a house,
Against the envy of less happier lands,
**QA (Glorifyingly)** This blessed plot, this earth, this realm, this
England,

# THE HISTORIES – WOMEN 133

**PG (I Push) QA (Hurtfully)** This nurse, this teeming womb of royal
  kings,
Fear'd by their breed and famous by their birth,
Renowned for their deeds as far from home,
For Christian service and true chivalry,
As is the sepulchre in stubborn Jewry,
Of the world's ransom, blessed Mary's Son,
This land of such dear souls, this dear dear land,
Dear for her reputation through the world,
Is now leased out, I die pronouncing it,
Like to a tenement or pelting farm.
**PG (I Penetrate) QA (Accusingly)** England, bound in with the tri-
  umphant sea
Whose rocky shore beats back the envious siege
Of watery Neptune, is now bound in with shame,
With inky blots and rotten parchment bonds:
That England, that was wont to conquer others,
Hath made a shameful conquest of itself.
**PG (I Close) QA (Wishfully)** Ah, would the scandal vanish with my
  life,
How happy then were my ensuing death!] *End AF 2*

**Note: This speech is for a mature person. John of Gaunt is on his
deathbed and he means to speak his mind to hopefully change others.
Young folks should work on and appreciate the poetry within yet, stay
away from it for an audition. It is long and difficult unless one can
really commit to the QA changes.**

## Two

*Richard II*
Act III, sc. ii

King Richard—AR—King, Child Divine, Poet, Diplomat, Victim

### *AF 1*

PG/AC = I Smash/I Demand.
QA = Harshly

134 THE HISTORIES – WOMEN

BP = The Treatise of Kings

OB = I want to live and be treated as a kind human being and not
a God.

AM = Mad

OS = Treating Kings as normal is not what is expected.

CX = Major (building)

ST = Life and death.


**AF (Victim)** [No matter where; of comfort no man speak.

**AM (Sad) PG (I Open) QA (Sorrowfully)** Let's talk of graves, of
worms, and epitaphs;

Make dust our paper and with rainy eyes

Write sorrow on the bosom of the earth.

**QA (What-the-hell-ly)** Let's choose executors and talk of wills:

**QA (Plainly)** And yet not so, for what can we bequeath

Save our deposed bodies to the ground?

**PG (I Close) QA (Surrenderingly)** Our lands, our lives and all are
Bolingbroke's,

And nothing can we call our own but death

And that small model of the barren earth

Which serves as paste and cover to our bones.

**PG (I Push) QA (Hurriedly)** For God's sake, let us sit upon the ground

And tell sad stories of the death of kings—

**PG (I Close) QA (Guiltily)** How some have been deposed; some
slain in war,

**QA (Affrightedly)** Some haunted by the ghosts they have deposed;

Some poison'd by their wives, some sleeping kill'd;


**Note: When you have a phrase as above consider dividing each part,
between punctuation, with a rise in pitch. In other words, part one
would be in your lowest register, part two is somewhat higher in pitch
and the last the highest in pitch but not necessarily the highest in your
register. This will give you changes without having to alter your QA.**


**QA (Bottom-line-ed-ly)** All murder'd. **PG (I Lift) QA (Truthfully)**
For within the hollow

crown

That rounds the mortal temples of a king

Keeps Death his court and there the antic sits,

THE HISTORIES – WOMEN 135

Scoffing his state and grinning at his pomp,
Allowing him a breath, a little scene,
To monarchize, be fear'd and kill with looks,
Infusing him with self and vain conceit,
As if this flesh which walls about our life,
Were brass impregnable, and humour'd thus
Comes at the last and with a little pin
Bores through his castle wall, **QA (Undoubtedly)** and farewell king!
**PG (I Open) QA (Relinquishingly)** Cover your heads and mock not
    flesh and blood
With solemn reverence. Throw away respect,
Tradition, form and ceremonious duty,
For you have but mistook me all this while:
I live with bread like you, feel want,
Taste grief, need friends: **PG (I Embrace) QA (Forsakenly)** sub-
    jected thus,
How can you say to me, I am a king?] *End AF 1*

**Note: This is a very famous speech, the 'Hollow Crown,' and is often
done at auditions. If you choose to use this monologue as an audition
piece, I suggest you take your time and make sure you nail your QA's—
whatever they are. This is a highly emotional speech that Richard
somewhat 'veils' until the end.**

# Three

*Richard II*
Act III, sc. iii

King Richard—AR—King, Child Divine, Poet, Diplomat, Victim

## MONOLOGUE

### *AF 1*

PG/AC = I Close/I Reflect
**Note: One can actively reflect.**
QA = Despairingly
BP = The Naked Truth

136 THE HISTORIES – WOMEN

OB = I want to live—even if it means not being a King.
AM = Sad
OS = Bolingbroke may have other ideas.
CX = Major (building)
ST = Life or Death


**AR (Victim)** [What must the King do now? Must he submit?
The king shall do it. Must he be deposed?

**Note: Much like the note for long phrases consider rising in pitch after
each question—unless there is a QA change.**

**PG (I Open) QA (Resolvedly)** The king shall be contented. **QA
(Despairingly)** Must he lose
The name of King? **QA (Resolvedly)** I' God's name, let it go.
**QA (Promisingly)** I'll give my jewels for a set of beads,
My gorgeous palace for a hermitage,
My gay apparel for an almsman's gown,
My figured goblets for a dish of wood,
My sceptre for a palmer's walking staff,
My subjects for a pair of carved saints
And my large kingdom for a little grave,
**QA (Despairingly)** A little, little grave, an obscure grave;
Or I'll be buried in the King's highway,
Some way of common trade, where subjects' feet
May hourly trample on their sovereign's head;
**QA (Why-not-ed-ly)** For on my heart they tread now whilst I live;
And buried once, why not upon my head?
**PG (I Embrace) QA (Sorrowfully—I feel sorry for)** Aumerle, thou
weep'st, my tender-hearted
cousin!
We'll make foul weather with despised tears;
Our sighs and they shall lodge the summer corn,
And make a dearth in this revolting land.
**QA (Playfully)** Or shall we play the wantons with our woes,
And make some pretty match with shedding tears?
As thus, to drop them still upon one place,
Till they have fretted us a pair of graves
Within the earth; and, therein laid,—there lies

# THE HISTORIES – WOMEN 137

Two kinsmen digg'd their graves with weeping eyes.
Would not this ill do well? Well, well, I see
I talk but idly, and you laugh at me.
**QA (I Penetrate) QA (Sarcastically)** Most mighty prince, my Lord
   Northumberland,
What says King Bolingbroke? Will his majesty
Give Richard leave to live till Richard die?
You make a leg, and Bolingbroke says ay.

**Note: There are a couple of ways to interpret the beginning of this
monologue. I chose, in my exploration, to save any sarcasm to the very
end. Is there another path for you to choose? It depends on how you view
your relationship with York—Richard's cousin—to whom he is speaking.**

## Four

*Richard II*
Act IV, sc. i

Bishop of Carlisle—AR—Disciple, Child Divine, Prophet, Puritan,
   Warrior

## MONOLOGUE

### *AF 1*

PG/AC = I Push/I Articulate (the truth)
QA = Modestly
BP = The Divine Right
OB = I want Richard to remain King.
AM = Mad
OS = Bolingbroke and his forces.
CX = Major (building)
ST = Bolingbroke threatens not only the rule of England but the
   Church as well.

**AR (Prophet)** [Worst in this royal presence may I speak,
Yet best beseeming me to speak the truth.

## 138 THE HISTORIES – WOMEN

**QA (Admonishingly)** Would God that any in this noble presence
Were enough noble to be upright judge
Of noble Richard! Then true noblesse would
Learn him forbearance from so foul a wrong.
**PG (I Penetrate) QA (Caution-ing-ly)** What subject can give sentence on his King?
And who sits here that is not Richard's subject?
**PG (I Open) QA (Judgingly)** Thieves are not judged but they are
  by to hear,
Although apparent guilt be seen in them;
And shall the figure of God's majesty,
His captain, steward, deputy-elect,
Anointed, crowned, planted many years,
Be judged by subject and inferior breath,
And he himself not present? **QA (Pleadingly)** O, forfend it, God,
That in a Christian climate souls refined
Should show so heinous, black, obscene a deed!
**PG (I Push) QA (Calmly)** I speak to subjects, and a subject speaks,
Stirr'd up by God, thus boldly for his king.
**PG (I Wring) QA (Warningly)** My Lord of Hereford here, whom
  you call king,

**Note: Once again, build carefully and with volume and pitch.**

Is a foul traitor to proud Hereford's king,
And if you crown him, let me prophesy:
The blood of English shall manure the ground,
And future ages groan for this foul act;
Peace shall go sleep with Turks and infidels,
And in this seat of peace tumultuous wars
Shall kin with kin and kind with kind confound;
Disorder, horror, fear and mutiny
Shall here inhabit, and this land be call'd
The field of Golgotha and dead men's skulls.
**PG (I Close) QA (Woefully)** O, if you raise this house against this house,
It will the woefullest division prove
That ever fell upon this cursed earth.
**PG (I Embrace) (Bottom-of-my-soul-ly)** Prevent it, resist it, let it
  not be so,
Lest child, child's children, cry against you woe!] *End AF 1*

# THE HISTORIES – WOMEN

**Note: This is a speech not often done at auditions. Keep in mind the high stakes and remain in control and it will be a wonderful audition piece.**

## Five

*Henry IV, Pt. 1*
Act I, sc. iii

Hotspur—AR—Warrior, Child Divine, Lover, Provocateur

## MONOLOGUE

PG/AC = I Smash/I Defend
QA = Vehemently
BP = The True Story
OB = I want the King to know the truth.
AM = Mad
OS = The King has denied me (our family) before.
CX = Major (building)
ST = Gaining or losing the favor of the King.

**AR (Warrior)** [My liege, I did deny no prisoners.
**PG (I Tear) QA (By-God-ly)** But I remember, when the fight was done,

**Note: As a rehearsal tool you can articulate the QA 'By-God-ly' before you say the words in the speech. So—it would read—By God, but I remember, when the fight was done . . . through to the next QA. Work to maintain the QA throughout. Use this technique with any QA you may have difficulty making clear.**

When I was dry with rage and extreme toil,
Breathless and faint, leaning upon my sword,
Came there a certain lord, **QA (Disgustingly)** neat, and trimly
    dress'd,
Fresh as a bridegroom; and his chin new reap'd,
Show'd like a stubble-land at harvest-home.
**PG (I Open) QA (Unbelievingly)** He was perfumed like a milliner;
And 'twixt his finger and his thumb he held
A pouncet-box, which ever and anon

# 140                    THE HISTORIES – WOMEN

He gave his nose and took't away again;
Who therewith angry, when it next came there,
Took it in snuff; and still he smiled and talk'd,
**PG (I Wring) QA (Angrily)** And as the soldiers bore dead bodies by,
He call'd them untaught knaves, unmannerly,
To bring a slovenly unhandsome corse
Betwixt the wind and his nobility.
With many holiday and lady terms
He question'd me; amongst the rest, demanded
My prisoners in your majesty's behalf.
**PG (I Open) QA (Apologetically)** I then, all smarting with my
     wounds being cold,
**QA (Sarcastically)** To be so pester'd with a popinjay,
**QA (Apologetically)** Out of my grief and my impatience,
Answer'd neglectingly I know not what,
He should or he should not; **QA (Angrily)** for he made me mad
To see him shine so brisk and smell so sweet
And talk so like a waiting-gentlewoman
Of guns and drums and wounds—God save the mark!—
**PG (I Embrace) QA (Appealingly—to appeal to the King)** And tell-
     ing me the sovereign'st
thing on earth
Was parmaceti for an inward bruise;
And that it was great pity, so it was,
This villanous salt-petre should be digg'd
Out of the bowels of the harmless earth,
Which many a good tall fellow had destroy'd
So cowardly; and but for these vile guns,
He would himself have been a soldier.
**PG (I Open) QA (Pledge-ing-ly)** This bald unjointed chat of his,
     my lord,
I answer'd indirectly, as I said;
And I beseech you, let not his report
Come current for an accusation
Betwixt my love and your high majesty.] *End AF 1*


**Note: Hotspur has quite a temper. Allow the temper to manifest as
inner tempo. Keep your outer tempo in check. If your temper is**

# THE HISTORIES – WOMEN 141

properly controlled the audience will know your inner tempo and go on the Rhythmical Wave roller-coaster with you.

## Six

*Henry IV, Pt. II*
Act III, sc. i

King Henry IV—AR—King, Child Divine, Warrior, Father (Patriarch)

## SOLILOQUY

### *AF 1*

PG/AC = I Open/I Reveal
QA = Frustratingly
BP = The Heavy Crown
OB = I want support (from my subjects—the audience.)

**Note: Henry enlisted common people in his armies. The immediate OB might be 'I want to sleep to forget the coming day.' Yet, remember that soliloquies are most often asking for the audience to be on your side and for help. Allow the audience's radiation to motivate you.**

AM = Mad
OS = Time
CX = Major (building)
ST = My kingdom may fall tomorrow.

**AR (King)** [How many thousand of my poorest subjects
Are at this hour asleep! **AM (Sad) QA (Exasperatedly)** O sleep, O
    gentle sleep,
Nature's soft nurse, how have I frighted thee,
That thou no more wilt weigh my eyelids down
And steep my senses in forgetfulness?
**QA (Puzzlingly)** Why rather, sleep, liest thou in smoky cribs,
Upon uneasy pallets stretching thee
And hush'd with buzzing night-flies to thy slumber,

142 THE HISTORIES – WOMEN

Than in the perfumed chambers of the great,
Under the canopies of costly state,
And lull'd with sound of sweetest melody?
**AM (Mad) PG (I Smash) QA (Heatedly)** O thou dull god, why liest
thou with the vile
In loathsome beds, and leavest the kingly couch
A watch-case or a common 'larum-bell?
**QA (Challengingly)** Wilt thou upon the high and giddy mast
Seal up the ship-boy's eyes, and rock his brains
In cradle of the rude imperious surge
And in the visitation of the winds,
Who take the ruffian billows by the top,
Curling their monstrous heads and hanging them
With deafening clamour in the slippery clouds,
That, with the hurly, death itself awakes?
**PG (I Close) QA (Remarkably)** Canst thou, O partial sleep, give
thy repose
To the wet sea-boy in an hour so rude,
And in the calmest and most stillest night,
With all appliances and means to boot,
Deny it to a king? **AM (Mad) PG (I Smash) QA (Angrily)** Then
happy low, lie down!
**AM (Sad) PG (I Close) QA (Dejectedly)** Uneasy lies the head that
wears a crown.] *End AF 1*

**Note: Henry is in a real pickle. He is threatened by the French armies,
the rebellion of Scots in the west, and the nobles of his own realm are
rebelling. Anyone would have trouble sleeping. The stakes are high
indeed and you must invest in them and all the while the circumstances
of lack of sleep are weighing on you. This is a very interesting speech
to work on from those perspectives. It requires balance.**

## Seven

*Henry IV, Pt. II*
Act IV, sc. v

Prince Hal—AR—Prince, Child Divine, Rebel, Warrior, Seeker,
Liberator

# MONOLOGUE

## *AF 1*

PG/AC = I Embrace/I Declare
QA = Pleadingly
BP = The Oath
OB = I want my father's love and blessing.
AM = Sad
OS = Father is on his deathbed.
CX = Major (building)
ST = My father may die not knowing the truth.


**AR (Child Divine)** [O, pardon me, my liege! But for my tears,
The moist impediments unto my speech,
I had forestall'd this dear and deep rebuke
Ere you with grief had spoke and I had heard
The course of it so far. **QA (Loyally)** There is your crown;
And He that wears the crown immortally
Long guard it yours! **QA (Promisingly)** If I affect it more
Than as your honour and as your renown,
Let me no more from this obedience rise,
Which my most inward true and duteous spirit
Teacheth, this prostrate and exterior bending.
**QA (Swear-to-God-ed-ly)** God witness with me, when I here came in,
And found no course of breath within your majesty,
How cold it struck my heart! If I do feign,
O, let me in my present wildness die
And never live to show the incredulous world
The noble change that I have purposed!
**PG (I Open) QA (Purposefully)** Coming to look on you, thinking
   you dead,
And dead almost, my liege, to think you were,
I spake unto this crown as having sense,
And thus upbraided it: 'The care on thee depending
Hath fed upon the body of my father;
Therefore, thou best of gold art worst of gold:
Other, less fine in carat, is more precious,
Preserving life in medicine potable;
But thou, most fine, most honour'd: most renown'd,

144 THE HISTORIES – WOMEN

Hast eat thy bearer up.' **QA (Confessedly)** Thus, my most royal
    liege,
Accusing it, I put it on my head,
To try with it, as with an enemy
That had before my face murder'd my father,
The quarrel of a true inheritor.
**PG (I Embrace) QA (Faithfully)** But if it did infect my blood with
    joy,
Or swell my thoughts to any strain of pride;
If any rebel or vain spirit of mine
Did with the least affection of a welcome
Give entertainment to the might of it,
Let God for ever keep it from my head
And make me as the poorest vassal is
That doth with awe and terror kneel to it!

**Note: It is often said there is no subtext in Shakespeare. There is some
validity in that thought in that, for the most part, characters say what
they mean and mean what they say. In this speech there is certainly
no subtext. Hal is destroyed emotionally knowing his father may die
mistakenly thinking that Hal seeks only the crown and does not love
him. So—the tricky part is to keep your emotion from boiling over.
Again, it is a matter of balance.**

## Eight

*Henry V*
Act I, sc. ii

King Henry V—AR—King, Child Divine, Rebel, Warrior, Seeker,
    Liberator

## MONOLOGUE

### *AF 1*

PG/AC = I Wring/I Squeeze
QA = Sarcastically

# THE HISTORIES – WOMEN

**145**

BP = The Message
OB = I want to send a clear message to the Dauphin.
AM = Mad
OS = A war must be fought first.
CX = Major (building)
ST = Binding of two nations under English rule.


**AR (King)** [We are glad the Dauphin is so pleasant with us;
His present and your pains we thank you for:
When we have march'd our rackets to these balls,
We will, in France, by God's grace, play a set
Shall strike his father's crown into the hazard.
**QA (Piercingly)** Tell him he hath made a match with such a
     wrangler
That all the courts of France will be disturb'd
With chases. **QA (Coolly)** And we understand him well,
How he comes o'er us with our wilder days,
Not measuring what use we made of them.
We never valued this poor seat of England;
And therefore, living hence, did give ourself
To barbarous licence; as 'tis ever common
That men are merriest when they are from home.
**QA (Hotly)** But tell the Dauphin I will keep my state,
Be like a king and show my sail of greatness
When I do rouse me in my throne of France.
**QA (Gloriously)** For that I have laid by my majesty
And plodded like a man for working-days,
But I will rise there with so full a glory
That I will dazzle all the eyes of France,
Yea, strike the Dauphin blind to look on us.
**QA (Reservedly)** And tell the pleasant prince this mock of his
Hath turn'd his balls to gun-stones; and his soul
Shall stand sore charged for the wasteful vengeance
That shall fly with them: **QA (Promisingly)** for many a thousand
     widows
Shall this his mock mock out of their dear husbands;
Mock mothers from their sons, mock castles down;
And some are yet ungotten and unborn

150                    THE HISTORIES – WOMEN

That shall have cause to curse the Dauphin's scorn.
**QA (Vengefully)** But this lies all within the will of God,
To whom I do appeal; and in whose name
Tell you the Dauphin I am coming on,
To venge me as I may and to put forth
My rightful hand in a well-hallow'd cause.
**QA (Difficultly)** So get you hence in peace; **(Resolvedly)** and tell
the Dauphin
His jest will savour but of shallow wit,
When thousands weep more than did laugh at it.
Convey them with safe conduct. **QA (Fuck-you-ed-ly)** Fare you
well.] *End AF 1*

**Note: When working with only one PG for the entire speech it is a good idea to build it with tempo and intensity. Sometimes we 'Squeeze' hard and then back off a bit. Nonetheless, we are always 'Squeezing.' You can always reinvest in the PG as you rehearse.**

## Nine

*Henry V*
Act IV, sc. iii

King Henry V—AR—King, Child Divine, Rebel, Warrior, Seeker,
Liberator

### MONOLOGUE

### *AF 1*

PG/AC = I Embrace/I Motivate
QA = Proudly
BP = The Reason (to fight and win)
OB = I want the army to fight with all its will (to win.)
AM = Glad
OS = The French army.
CX = Major
ST = Life or death for all of us and England.

**AR (Warrior)** [This day is called the feast of Crispian:
He that outlives this day, and comes safe home,
Will stand a tip-toe when the day is named,
And rouse him at the name of Crispian.
**QA (Brotherly)** He that shall live this day, and see old age,
Will yearly on the vigil feast his neighbours,
And say 'To-morrow is Saint Crispian.'
Then will he strip his sleeve and show his scars,
And say 'These wounds I had on Crispin's day.'
**QA (Factually)** Old men forget; yet all shall be forgot,
But he'll remember with advantages
What feats he did that day: **QA (Proudly)** then shall our names,
Familiar in his mouth as household words
Harry the king, Bedford and Exeter,
Warwick and Talbot, Salisbury and Gloucester,
Be in their flowing cups freshly remember'd.
**QA (Historically)** This story shall the good man teach his son;
And Crispin Crispian shall ne'er go by,
From this day to the ending of the world,
But we in it shall be remember'd;
**QA (Brotherly)** We few, we happy few, we band of brothers;
For he to-day that sheds his blood with me
Shall be my brother; be he ne'er so vile,
This day shall gentle his condition:
**QA (Gloriously)** And gentlemen in England now a-bed
Shall think themselves accursed they were not here,
And hold their manhoods cheap whiles any speaks
That fought with us upon Saint Crispin's day.] *End AF 1*

**Note: Think back to the speech spoken by Chorus at the beginning of
this play. You really need to reach into your imagination to get to the
stakes of this speech. The armies of France outnumber the English.
Henry is motivating his troops before the fight. From your imagination
springs this monologue. Henry, former Prince Hal, is full of 'piss and
vinegar.' Yet, look at the punctuation—nary an exclamation mark to be
found. This should tell you that King Henry is controlling his emotions
outwardly. Inwardly, he must be experiencing fear, anger, and great
excitement. This is a great speech for inner/outer tempo.**

# 148       THE HISTORIES – WOMEN

## Ten

*Richard III*
Act I, sc. i

Richard—AR—Prince, King, Child Divine, Tyrant, Politician, Predator

## SOLILOQUY

PG/AC = I Open/I Rejoice
QA = Happily
BP = The Victory (over the Lancasters)
OB = I want to celebrate my victory.
AM = Glad
OS = I have some moves to make before I can be King.
CX = Auxiliary
ST = All moves must be carefully calculated or I could be beheaded.

**AR (Politician)** [Now is the winter of our discontent
Made glorious summer by this sun of York;
And all the clouds that lour'd upon our house
In the deep bosom of the ocean buried.
**QA (Victoriously)** Now are our brows bound with victorious wreaths;
Our bruised arms hung up for monuments;
**QA (Merrily)** Our stern alarums changed to merry meetings,
**QA (Dreadfully)** Our dreadful marches **QA (Delightfully)** to delightful measures.
**QA (Peacefully)** Grim-visaged war hath smooth'd his wrinkled front;
And now, instead of mounting barbed steeds
To fright the souls of fearful adversaries,
**PG (I Close) QA (Boringly)** He capers nimbly in a lady's chamber

**Note: The turn in attitude is interesting. There could be a level of sarcasm throughout the first part of the soliloquy. Yet, I didn't find; in my exploration, that sarcasm helped my objective in any way. Still, it could be there closely 'veiled.' It is also a valid choice**

# THE HISTORIES – WOMEN                    149

**to wait for the turn in the next AF. Play with both and come to your own conclusions.**

**Chekhov teaches us, in his Laws of Composition, that the beginning of the play exists in its ending and vice-versa. Look near the end of this speech and note the line, 'And hate the idle pleasures of these days. . . ' This turn is based on that principle.**

To the lascivious pleasing of a lute.] *End AF 1*

## *AF 2*

PG/AC = I Lift/I Unveil
QA = Okay-ly (It's O.K.)
BP = The Simple Facts
OB = I want to be King.
AM = Same
OS = Same
CX = Major (building)
ST = Same

**AR (Tyrant)** [But I, that am not shaped for sportive tricks,
Nor made to court an amorous looking-glass;
**QA (Irritatingly-slightly)** I, that am rudely stamp'd, and want love's
    majesty
To strut before a wanton ambling nymph;
**QA (Begrudgingly)** I, that am curtail'd of this fair proportion,
Cheated of feature by dissembling nature,
Deformed, unfinish'd, sent before my time
Into this breathing world, scarce half made up,
And that so lamely and unfashionable
That dogs bark at me as I halt by them;
**QA (Piss-off-ed-ly)** Why, I, in this weak piping time of peace,
Have no delight to pass away the time,
Unless to spy my shadow in the sun
And descant on mine own deformity.
**QA (Openly)** And therefore, since I cannot prove a lover,
To entertain these fair well-spoken days,
I am determined to prove a villain
And hate the idle pleasures of these days.
**QA (Calculatingly)** Plots have I laid, inductions dangerous,

150          THE HISTORIES – WOMEN

By drunken prophecies, libels and dreams,
To set my brother Clarence and the King
In deadly hate the one against the other:
**QA (Hopefully)** And if King Edward be as true and just
As I am subtle, false and treacherous,
This day should Clarence closely be mew'd up,
About a prophecy, which says that 'G'
Of Edward's heirs the murderer shall be.
**PG (I Smash) QA (Veiledly)** Dive, thoughts, down to my soul: here
Clarence comes.] *End AF 2*

**Note: There are many ways to approach this speech. This is simply the one I settled on in my process. It's so interesting that Richard admits to being a villain. No other villain in history admits so—even Adolph Hitler. Given this it does sway one's choices for there is very little to veil. Richard has absolutely no moral compass. In the case of Hitler— he thought he was making the world a better place. There is a different driving force in play here. The kicker of it all—the audience likes Richard . . . to a certain extent. If you really delve into the language of this speech, especially the vowel sounds, you'll begin to understand why the audience likes Richard, or at least is extremely intrigued by him. Speech, however, is not the focus of this book. But you'd better pay attention to it as an equal to this work.**

## Eleven

*Richard III*
Act I, sc. ii

Richard—AR—Prince, King, Child Divine, Tyrant, Politician, Predator

## SOLILOQUY

### *AF 1*

PG/AC = I Embrace/I Gloat
QA = Giddily

# THE HISTORIES – WOMEN                    151

BP = The Slam Dunk
OB = I want to bask in my success on my journey to be King.
AM = Glad
OS = The marriage is not yet sealed.
CX = Major (building)
ST = <u>My</u> kingdom!


**AR (Predator)** [Was ever woman in this humour woo'd?
Was ever woman in this humour won?
I'll have her; **QA (Brutally)** but I will not keep her long.
**QA (Unbelievingly)** What! I, that kill'd her husband and his father,
To take her in her heart's extremest hate,
With curses in her mouth, **QA (Mockingly)** tears in her eyes,
**QA (Boastfully)** The bleeding witness of her hatred by;
Having God, her conscience, and these bars against me,
And I nothing to back my suit at all,
But the plain devil and dissembling looks,
And yet to win her, all the world to nothing!
**QA (Celebratorily)** Ha!
**QA (Laughingly)** Hath she forgot already that brave prince,
Edward, her lord, whom I, some three months since,
Stabb'd in my angry mood at Tewksbury?
**QA (Sarcastically)** A sweeter and a lovelier gentleman,
Framed in the prodigality of nature,
Young, valiant, wise, and, no doubt, right royal,
The spacious world cannot again afford
**QA (Unbelievingly)** And will she yet debase her eyes on me,
That cropp'd the golden prime of this sweet prince,
And made her widow to a woeful bed?
On me, whose all not equals Edward's moiety?
On me, that halt and am unshapen thus?
**PG (I Open) QA (Feign Egotistically)** My dukedom to a beggarly
       denier,
I do mistake my person all this while!
Upon my life, she finds, although I cannot,
Myself to be a marvellous proper man.
**QA (Bitterly)** I'll be at charges for a looking-glass,
And entertain some score or two of tailors,

152 THE HISTORIES – WOMEN

To study fashions to adorn my body:
But first I'll turn yon fellow in his grave;
And then return lamenting to my love.
Shine out, fair sun, till I have bought a glass,
That I may see my shadow as I pass.] *End AF 1*

**Note: As with any speech there is always interpretation. You may notice that this speech begins with the QA 'giddily' and ends with the QA 'bitterly.' I followed Chekhov's Laws of Composition using this concept of Polarity. This concept tells us that the beginning of the play, in this case speech, should transform itself into its opposite at the end. Just this one simple idea helps give the play, or speech, a simple way to create a dynamic Rhythmical Wave. It's a great idea to work on the beginning and then the ending and then proceed to the middle. Guiding your QA's in between the two will aid in creating a pathway that is vigorous and energetic. In your exploration always look for opposite QA's.**

## Twelve

*Richard III*
Act II, sc. i

King Edward IV—AR—King, Child Divine, Victim, Politician

## MONOLOGUE

### *AF 1*

PG/AC = I Push
QA = Angrily
BP = The Bad News
OB = I want God to know I tried to save Clarence.
AM = Mad
OS = Time (too late to save Clarence)
CX = Major (building)
ST = Justice (See last three lines.)

**AR (Victim)** [Have I a tongue to doom my brother's death,
And shall the same give pardon to a slave?

# THE HISTORIES – WOMEN

**AM (Sad) PG (I Close) QA (Bitterly)** My brother slew no man; his
  fault was thought,
And yet his punishment was cruel death.
**AM (Mad) PG (I Push) QA (Accusingly)** Who sued to me for him?
  Who, in my rage,
Kneel'd at my feet, and bade me be advised?
**PG (I Close) QA (Brotherly)** Who spake of brotherhood? **QA
  (Lovingly)** Who spake of love?
**PG (I Open) QA (Accusingly)** Who told me how the poor soul did
  forsake
The mighty Warwick, and did fight for me?
**PG (I Close) QA (Difficultly)** Who told me, in the field by
  Tewksbury
When Oxford had me down, he rescued me,
And said, 'Dear brother, live, and be a king'?
**PG (I Embrace) QA (Desperately)** Who told me, when we both lay
  in the field
Frozen almost to death, how he did lap me
Even in his own garments, and gave himself,
All thin and naked, to the numb cold night?
**PG (I Smash) QA (Hatefully-filled with hate)** All this from my re-
  membrance brutish wrath
Sinfully pluck'd, and not a man of you
Had so much grace to put it in my mind.
But when your carters or your waiting-vassals
Have done a drunken slaughter, and defaced
The precious image of our dear Redeemer,
You straight are on your knees for pardon, pardon;
And I unjustly too, must grant it you.
**PG (I Open) QA (Woefully)** But for my brother not a man would
  speak,
Nor I, ungracious, speak unto myself
For him, poor soul. The proudest of you all
Have been beholding to him in his life;
Yet none of you would once plead for his life.
**QA (Fearfully)** O God, I fear thy justice will take hold
On me, and you, and mine, and yours for this.
**QA (Commandingly)** Come Hastings, help me to my closet. **QA
  (Emptily)** Oh, poor Clarence!

**Note: This is quite a lovely monologue and is not overdone. One of the reasons it is not often done is the fact that Edward is dying, and folks think the speech doesn't work out of context of the play. Not so. The audience, and casting folk, know that Edward is dying. It is a simple circumstance of the play. Don't worry about that. Just play what you can play—Actions and Qualities of Action. You definitely can't play dying.**

### End Chapter Five

Other speeches to consider from the Histories (Index of First Lines)

1. *King John*
   Act I, sc. i
   Philip the Bastard—'Brother, adieu. Good fortune come to thee. . .'

2. *King John*
   Act II, sc. i
   Philip the Bastard—'Mad world, mad kings, mad composition!'

3. *King John*
   Act III, sc. i
   Constance—'If thou that bidst me be content wert grim. . .'

4. *King John*
   Act III, sc. iv
   Constance—'Lo now! Now; see the issue of your peace!'

5. *King John*
   Act V, sc. ii
   Lewis—'Your Grace shall pardon me, I will not back.'

6. *King John*
   Act V, sc. ii
   Philip the Bastard—'By all the blood that ever fury breathed. . .'

7. *Henry IV, Pt. I*
   Act V, sc. i
   Falstaff—'Tis not due yet—I would be loath to pay him. . .'

8. *Henry IV, Pt. II*
   Act II, sc. i
   Mistress Quickly—'Marry, if thou wert an honest man, thyself and the. . .'

# THE HISTORIES – WOMEN

9. *Henry IV, Pt. II*
Act IV, sc. iii
Falstaff—'I would you had but the wit—'twere better than. . . '

10. *Henry V*
Act V, sc. ii
King Henry V—'Fair Katherine, and most fair. . . '

11. *Henry VI, Pt. I*
Act V, Sc. iii
Joan la Pucelle—'The Regent conquers, and the Frenchmen fly.'

12. *Henry VI, Pt. II*
Act I, sc. iii
Queen Margaret—'My Lord of Suffolk, say, is this the guise. . . '

13. *Henry VI, Pt. III*
Act II, sc. v
King Henry VI—'The battle fares like to the morning's war. . . '

14. *Richard III*
Act IV, sc. i
Lady Anne—'No? Why? When he that is my husband now. . . '

15. *Richard III*
Act IV, sc. iv
Margaret—'If ancient sorrow be most reverend. . . '

16. *Richard III*
Act V, sc. iii
King Richard—'Give me another horse! Bind up my wounds!'

# Chapter Six

# THE ROMANCES AND PROBLEM PLAYS – WOMEN

## *Romances*

### One

*Cymbeline*
Act III, sc. vi

Imogen—AR—Princess, Child Divine, Victim, Lover

### SOLILOQUY

### *AF 1*

PG/AC = I Pull/I Woman Up
QA = Resolvedly
BP = The Lost Lover
OB = I want to find my way to Milford Haven.
AM = Fear
OS = I'm lost.
CX = Major (building)
ST = I could die out here.


**AR (Lover)** [I see a man's life is a tedious one.
I have tired myself, and for two nights together
Have made the ground my bed. I should be sick,
But that my resolution helps me. **QA (Confusedly)** Milford,
When from the mountain-top Pisanio show'd thee,
Thou wast within a ken. **QA (Exasperatedly)** O Jove! I think

# THE ROMANCES AND PROBLEM PLAYS – WOMEN     157

Foundations fly the wretched; such, I mean,
Where they should be relieved. Two beggars told me
I could not miss my way: **QA (Quizzically)** will poor folks lie,
That have afflictions on them, knowing 'tis
A punishment or trial? **QA (Truthfully)** Yes; no wonder,
When rich ones scarce tell true. To lapse in fullness
Is sorer than to lie for need, and falsehood
Is worse in kings than beggars. **QA (I-get-it-ly)** My dear lord!
Thou art one o' the false ones. Now I think on thee,
My hunger's gone; but even before, I was
At point to sink for food. **QA (Discoveringly)** But what is this?
Here is a path to't: 'tis some savage hold:
**PG (I Close) QA (Fearfully)** I were best not to call; I dare not call.
    **QA (Steadfastly)** Yet
famine,
Ere clean it o'erthrow nature, makes it valiant,
Plenty and peace breeds cowards; hardness ever
Of hardiness is mother. **QA (Carefully)** Ho! who's here?
**PG (I Smash) QA (Challengingly)** If anything that's civil, speak; if
    savage,
Take or lend. Ho! **PG (I Lift) QA (Courageously)** No answer? Then
    I'll enter.
Best draw my sword: and if mine enemy
But fear the sword like me, he'll scarcely look on't.
Such a foe, good heavens!] *End AF 1*

**Note: Imogen is disguised as a man (another pants role) and has been
lost for two days. You need to research why her archetype is a Lover—
the key to the given circumstances.**

## Two

*The Winter's Tale*
Act III, sc. ii

Hermione—AR—Queen, Child Divine, Lover, Mother, Victim

# THE ROMANCES AND PROBLEM PLAYS – WOMEN

## MONOLOGUE

### *AF 1*

PG/AC = I Push/I Hold my Ground
QA = Contestingly
BP = The Defense
OB = I want Leontes to know the truth. I am innocent.
AM = Mad
OS = Leontes is convinced I am guilty.
CX = Major (building)
ST = Life or Death

**AR (Victim)** [Sir, spare your threats:
The bug which you would fright me with I seek.
To me can life be no commodity.
**PG (I Close) QA (Sadly)** The crown and comfort of my life, your favour,
I do give lost; for I do feel it gone,
But know not how it went. **QA (Missingly—she is separated from her son)** My second joy
And first-fruits of my body, from his presence
I am barr'd, like one infectious. **PG (I Push) QA (Bitterly)** My third comfort
Starr'd most unluckily, is from my breast,
The innocent milk in its most innocent mouth,
Haled out to murder; **PG (I Close) QA (Embarrassedly)** myself on every post
Proclaimed a strumpet; with immodest hatred
The child-bed privilege denied, which 'longs
To women of all fashion; **PG (I Penetrate) QA (Abashedly)** lastly, hurried
Here to this place, i' the open air, before
I have got strength of limit. **PG (I Open) QA (Do-what-you-will-ly)** Now, my liege,
Tell me what blessings I have here alive,
That I should fear to die? Therefore proceed.
**PG (I Penetrate) QA (Unwaveringly)** But yet hear this: mistake me not; no life,

# THE ROMANCES AND PROBLEM PLAYS – WOMEN    159

I prize it not a straw, but for mine honour,
Which I would free, if I shall be condemn'd
Upon surmises, all proofs sleeping else
But what your jealousies awake, I tell you
'Tis rigor and not law. **PG (I Open) QA (Daringly)** Your honours all,
I do refer me to the oracle:
Apollo be my judge!] *End AF 1*

## Three

*The Winter's Tale*
Act III, sc. ii

Paulina—AR—Companion, Child Divine, Victim

## MONOLOGUE

### *AF 1*

PG/AC = I Push/I Challenge
QA = Coolly (Veiled Anger)
BP = The Defense
OB = I want Leontes to see the error of his ways.
AM = Mad
OS = The King has already proven he is ready to kill.
CX = Major (building)
ST = Life or Death

**Note: Take care of the list in the beginning. Remember volume and pitch.**

**AR (Victim)** [What studied torments, tyrant, hast for me?
What wheels? Racks? Fires? What flaying? Boiling?
In leads or oils? What old or newer torture
Must I receive, whose every word deserves
To taste of thy most worst? **QA (Comparingly)** Thy tyranny
Together working with thy jealousies,
Fancies too weak for boys, too green and idle
For girls of nine, O, think what they have done

160    THE ROMANCES AND PROBLEM PLAYS – WOMEN

And then run mad indeed, stark mad! **PG (I Wring) QA (Accusingly)** For all

**Note: An even longer list. If you find more QA's that's great. In my rehearsal I found utilizing the rules of listing sufficed.**

Thy by-gone fooleries were but spices of it.
That thou betray'dst Polixenes, 'twas nothing;
That did but show thee, of a fool, inconstant
And damnable ingrateful. Nor was't much,
Thou wouldst have poison'd good Camillo's honour,
To have him kill a king; poor trespasses,
More monstrous standing by: whereof I reckon
The casting forth to crows thy baby-daughter
To be or none or little; though a devil
Would have shed water out of fire ere done't.
Nor is't directly laid to thee, the death
Of the young prince, whose honourable thoughts,
Thoughts high for one so tender, cleft the heart
That could conceive a gross and foolish sire
Blemish'd his gracious dam. **PG (I Open) QA (Heatedly)** This is
    not, no,
Laid to thy answer: but the last—O lords,
When I have said, cry 'woe!' The queen, the queen,
The sweet'st, dear'st creature's dead, and vengeance for't
Not dropp'd down yet.

## APPLICATION OF THE MICHAEL CHEKHOV TECHNIQUE TO SHAKESPEARE'S MONOLOGUES AND SOLILOQUIES

*THE ROMANCES AND PROBLEM PLAYS-MEN*

Romances

### One

*Cymbeline*
Act II, sc. ii

Iachimo—AR—Gambler, Child Eternal, Lover, Fool

# THE ROMANCES AND PROBLEM PLAYS – WOMEN    161

## MONOLOGUE

### *AF 1*

PG/AC = I Open  (I Justify—my long emergence in the trunk)
QA = Stealthily
BP = The Surprise
OB = I want 'evidence' of Imogen's infidelity.

**Note: This is a trick to win a bet placed with Posthumus.**

AM = Glad
OS = She may wake.
CX = Major (building)
ST = I stand to lose my entire estate.

**AR (Lover)** [The crickets sing, and man's o'er-labour'd sense
Repairs itself by rest. Our Tarquin thus
Did softly press the rushes, ere he waken'd
The chastity he wounded. **QA (Astonished)** Cytherea,
How bravely thou becomest thy bed, fresh lily,
And whiter than the sheets! **PG (I Embrace) QA (Carefully)** That
    I might touch!
**QA (Delicately)** But kiss; one kiss! **QA (Admiringly)** Rubies
    unparagon'd,
How dearly they do't! 'Tis her breathing that
Perfumes the chamber thus: the flame o' the taper
Bows toward her, and would under-peep her lids,
To see the enclosed lights, now canopied
Under these windows, white and azure laced
With blue of heaven's own tinct. **PG (I Close) QA (On-task-ly)** But
    my design,
To note the chamber. I will write all down:
Such and such pictures; there the window; such
The adornment of her bed; the arras; figures,
Why, such and such; and the contents o' the story.
**PG (I Penetrate) QA (Cautiously)** Ah, but some natural notes
    about her body,
Above ten thousand meaner moveables
Would testify, to enrich mine inventory.

# 162   THE ROMANCES AND PROBLEM PLAYS – WOMEN

**QA (Even-more-cautiously)** O sleep, thou ape of death, lie dull
upon her!

And be her sense but as a monument,

Thus in a chapel lying! Come off, come off. . .

*Taking off her bracelet*

**PG (I Close) QA (Relievedly)** As slippery as the Gordian knot was
hard!

**PG (I Open) QA (Victoriously)** 'Tis mine; and this will witness
outwardly,

As strongly as the conscience does within,

To the madding of her lord. **PG (I Penetrate) QA (Lustfully)** On
her left breast

A mole cinque-spotted, like the crimson drops

I' the bottom of a cowslip. **QA (Discoveringly)** Here's a voucher

Stronger than ever law could make. This secret

Will force him think I have pick'd the lock and ta'en

The treasure of her honour. **PG (I Close) QA (Nah-ly)** No more.
To what end?

Why should I write this down, that's riveted,

Screw'd to my memory? **PG (I Open) QA (Noticingly)** She hath
been reading late

The tale of Tereus; here the leaf's turn'd down

Where Philomel gave up. I have enough.

**PG (I Close) QA (Enough-ed-ly)** To the trunk again, and shut the
spring of it.

Swift, swift, you dragons of the night, that dawning

May bare the raven's eye! I lodge in fear;

Though this a heavenly angel, hell is here.

*Clock strikes*

One, two, three: time, time!] *End AF 1*

*Goes into the trunk. The scene closes*

---

**Note: To do this monologue full length would take well over two
minutes. So—as written, too long for an audition. We don't see it very
often because of that. Still, what a piece to work on! It can be very
comedic. There is the trunk to deal with. Iachimo has been in it for
hours. He has that to contend with as well as not waking Imogen. Work
on it and have fun with the possible 'silent-clown' type physicality.**

# THE ROMANCES AND PROBLEM PLAYS – WOMEN    163

## Two

*The Tempest*
Act II, sc. ii

Trinculo—AR—Fool, Child Orphan, Companion

## MONOLOGUE

### *AF 1*

PG/AC = I Tear/I Search
QA = Desperately
BP = The Storm Approaches
OB = I want to find a place to get out of the approaching storm.
AM = Fear
OS = The storm is approaching quickly.
CX = Major (building)
ST = The storm could be dangerous.
**AR (Fool)** [Here's neither bush nor shrub, to bear off
any weather at all, and another storm brewing;
I hear it sing i' the wind. **QA (Fearfully)** Yond same black
cloud, yond huge one, looks like a foul
bombard that would shed his liquor. If it
should thunder as it did before, I know not
where to hide my head; yond same cloud cannot
choose but fall by pailfuls. **PG (I Open) QA (Carefully)** What have we
here? A man or a fish? Dead or alive? **PG (I Close) QA (Disgustingly)** A fish:
he smells like a fish; a very ancient and fish-
like smell; a kind of not of the newest Poor-
John. **QA (Bewilderedly)** A strange fish! Were I in England now,
as once I was, and had but this fish painted,
not a holiday fool there but would give a piece
of silver: there would this monster make a
man; **PG (I Open) QA (Off-hand-ed-ly)** any strange beast there
makes a man:
**QA (Truthfully)** when they will not give a doit to relieve a lame

164 THE ROMANCES AND PROBLEM PLAYS – WOMEN

beggar, they will lazy out ten to see a dead
Indian. **QA (Curiously)** Legged like a man and his fins like
arms! **PG (I Pull—away) QA (Surprisingly)** Warm o' my troth! I do
now let loose
my opinion; hold it no longer: **QA (Realizingly)** this is no fish,
but an islander, that hath lately suffered by a thunderbolt.
*Thunder*
**PG (I Close) QA (Fearfully)** Alas, the storm is come again! My best
way is to
creep under his gaberdine; there is no other
shelter hereabouts: misery acquaints a man with
strange bed-fellows. I will here shroud till the
dregs of the storm be past.] *End AF 1*

**Note: This monologue may be overdone at auditions. With that said, it is rare to see an actor who has done his homework on fantasizing Caliban. I don't mean you have to do a great deal of work fantasizing what Caliban looks like. That part is easy. The work lies in the discovery of the new QA's and how they make you feel. Begin your work after discovering Caliban with your sense of smell and the QA's will sing out to you.**

# Three

*The Tempest*
Act III, sc. ii

Caliban—AR—Fool, Child Magical, Servant, Companion, Networker

## MONOLOGUE

### *AF 1*

PG/AC = I Penetrate/I Encourage
QA = Gleefully
BP = The Plot
OB = I want Prospero killed.

# THE ROMANCES AND PROBLEM PLAYS – WOMEN    165

AM = Glad

OS = Prospero is a magician. Hopefully he can't see into the future.

CX = Major

ST = I'm dead if Prospero discovers the plot.

**AR (Networker)** [Why, as I told thee, 'tis a custom with him,
I' th' afternoon to sleep. There thou mayst brain him,
**QA (Remindingly)** Having first seized his books, **QA (Gleefully)** or with a log
Batter his skull, or paunch him with a stake,
Or cut his wezand with thy knife. **QA (Remindingly)** Remember
First to possess his books; **PG (I Wring) QA (Informingly)** for without them
He's but a sot, as I am, nor hath not
One spirit to command: they all do hate him
As rootedly as I. **PG (I Penetrate) QA (Piercingly)** Burn but his books.
**PG (I Close) QA (Jealously)** He has brave utensils—for so he calls them—
Which when he has a house, he'll deck withal.
**PG (I Open) QA (Admiringly)** And that most deeply to consider is
The beauty of his daughter; **QA (Parenthetically 9)** he himself
Calls her a nonpareil: **PG (I Embrace) QA (Lovingly)** I never saw a woman,
But only Sycorax my dam and she;
But she as far surpasseth Sycorax
As great'st does least.] *End AF 1*

**Note: Caliban is enlisting help to kill Prospero and take Miranda, Prospero's daughter as his wife.**

## Four

*The Tempest*
Act IV, sc. i

Prospero—AR—Magician, Child Magical, Father, Victim, Wizard

# THE ROMANCES AND PROBLEM PLAYS – WOMEN

## MONOLOGUE

### *AF 1*

PG/AC = I Open/I Reveal
QA = Encouragingly
BP = The Life After
OB = I want to come to terms with my feelings.
AM = Glad

**Note: It's easy to interpret this speech with the atmosphere (subjective) of Sad. Yet, Prospero's plans are coming to fruition and he is glad of the way it all has turned out. There is some melancholy here. When we have a great plan that takes much of our time that comes out well there is a natural down period. My interpretation of the speech is more Glad than Sad. Perhaps yours will be different and that's all well.**

**It's good to know that Shakespeare is about to retire from the stage after many years of success. It has to feel bittersweet so the atmosphere might even be Bad. Bottom line is you are playing Prospero and not Shakespeare even though the poet is speaking personally through the main character. Take your time with the monologue. It is short and deeply meaningful.**

OS = Dealing with end of a long plan.
CX = Major (building)
ST = What's next?

**AR (Father)** [You do look, my son, in a moved sort,
As if you were dismay'd: be cheerful, sir.
Our revels now are ended. **QA (Assuredly)** These our actors,
As I foretold you, were all spirits and
Are melted into air, into thin air;
**QA (Prophetically)** And, like the baseless fabric of this vision,
The cloud-capp'd towers, the gorgeous palaces,
The solemn temples, **QA (Awesomely)** the great globe itself,
**QA (Prophetically)** Ye all which it inherit, shall dissolve
And, like this insubstantial pageant faded,
Leave not a rack behind. We are such stuff
As dreams are made on, and our little life
Is rounded with a sleep. **QA (Confession-ing-ly)** Sir, I am vex'd.
Bear with my weakness; my, brain is troubled.

**QA (Assuredly)** Be not disturb'd with my infirmity.
**QA (Invitingly)** If you be pleased, retire into my cell
And there repose. **QA (Resolvedly)** A turn or two I'll walk,
To still my beating mind.] *End AF 1*

Other speeches to consider from the Romances (Index of First Lines)

1. *Cymbeline*
   Act III, sc. ii
   Imogen—'Who, thy lord? That is my lord Leonatus?'

2. *Pericles*
   Act IV, sc. iii
   Dionyza—'She died at night; I'll say so. Who can cross it. . .'

3. *The Tempest*
   Act I, sc. ii
   Ariel—'All hail, great Master! Grave sir, hail! I come. . .'

4. *The Tempest*
   Act V, sc. i
   Prospero—'Ye elves of hills, brooks, standing lakes, and groves. . .'

5. *The Winter's Tale*
   Act III, sc. iii
   Shepard—'I would there were no age between ten and three. . .'

## THE PROBLEM PLAYS-WOMEN

## One

*All's Well That Ends Well*
Act III, sc. ii

Helena—AR—Princess, Child Divine, Lover, Victim

## SOLILOQUY

### *AF 1*

PG/AC = I Lift/I Realize
QA = Shockingly

BP = The Sacrifice

OB = I want to protect Bertram (Rossillion).

AM = Fear

OS = Bertram does not love or trust me.

CX = Major (building)

ST = Possible death if Bertram goes to battle.

**AR (Lover)** ['Till I have no wife, I have nothing in France.'
Nothing in France, until he has no wife!

**PG (I Close) QA (Resolvedly)** Thou shalt have none, Rousillon,
  none in France;

Then hast thou all again. **PG (I Embrace) QA (I Pity)** Poor lord!
  **PG (I Open) QA (Fearfully)**
Is't I
That chase thee from thy country and expose
Those tender limbs of thine to the event
Of the none-sparing war? And is it I
That drive thee from the sportive court, where thou
Wast shot at with fair eyes, to be the mark
Of smoky muskets? **PG (I Pull) QA (Prayerfully)** O you leaden
  messengers,
That ride upon the violent speed of fire,
Fly with false aim; move the still-peering air,
That sings with piercing; do not touch my lord.
**PG (I Close) QA (Guiltily)** Whoever shoots at him, I set him there;
Whoever charges on his forward breast,
I am the caitiff that do hold him to't;
And, though I kill him not, I am the cause
His death was so effected. **PG (I Embrace) QA (Acceptingly)** Better
  'twere
I met the ravin lion when he roar'd
With sharp constraint of hunger; better 'twere
That all the miseries which nature owes
Were mine at once. **PG (I Open) QA (Give-over-ed-ly)** No, come
  thou home, Rousillon,
Whence honour but of danger wins a scar,
As oft it loses all. I will be gone;
My being here it is that holds thee hence.
**PG (I Close) QA (Hesitantly)** Shall I stay here to do't? **PG (I Open)
  QA (Resolvedly)** No, no,

# THE ROMANCES AND PROBLEM PLAYS – WOMEN    169

although
The air of paradise did fan the house
And angels officed all. I will be gone,
That pitiful rumour may report my flight,
To consolate thine ear. **QA (Hopefully)** Come, night; end, day!
For with the dark, poor thief, I'll steal away.] *End AF 1*

**Note: Helena is married to Bertram, Count of Rossillion. He wants
nothing to do with her and has sent a letter stating so. Helena takes the
high road in this speech. She loves him so much, and doesn't want him
to go to war, that she resolves herself to back away.**

## Two

*Measure for Measure*
Act II, sc. ii

Isabella—AR—Virgin, Child Divine, Nun, Victim, Liberator

## MONOLOGUE

### *AF 1*

PG/AC = I Push/I Blame
QA = Accusatorily
BP = The Saving Grace
OB = I want Angelo to spare my brother's life.
AM = Fear
OS = Angelo has revised a law that has not been invoked in a long
    time.
CX = Major (building)
ST = Life or Death

**AR (Liberator)** [So you must be the first that gives this sentence,
And he, that suffer's. O, it is excellent
To have a giant's strength; but it is tyrannous
To use it like a giant.
*[Lucio, aside to Isabella . . . 'That's well said.']*
**AM (Mad) QA (Angrily)** Could great men thunder

# 170    THE ROMANCES AND PROBLEM PLAYS – WOMEN

As Jove himself does, Jove would ne'er be quiet,
For every pelting, petty officer
Would use his heaven for thunder;
Nothing but thunder! **QA (Exasperatedly)** Merciful Heaven,
Thou rather with thy sharp and sulphurous bolt
Split'st the unwedgeable and gnarled oak
Than the soft myrtle. **QA (Carefully)** But man, proud man,
Drest in a little brief authority,
Most ignorant of what he's most assured,
His glassy essence, like an angry ape,
Plays such fantastic tricks before high heaven
As make the angels weep; who, with our spleens,
Would all themselves laugh mortal.] *End AF 1*

**Note: Angelo has sentenced Isabella's brother to death under an antiquated law of having sex before marriage. Isabella comes before Angelo, the Duke's deputy, to plead for her brother's life. This is another speech during which you cannot afford to lose your temper. If you do, Angelo might decide to kill your brother today! Use inner/ outer tempo to accomplish your objective.**

## Three

*Troilus and Cressida*
Act III, sc. ii

Cressida—AR—Princess, Child Divine, Heroine, Victim, Lover

## MONOLOGUE

### *AF 1*

PG/AC = I Open/I Divulge
QA = Dizzily
BP = The Confession
OB = I want Troilus!
AM = Glad (Lust)
OS = Troilus may take too much for granted. (Equality)

# THE ROMANCES AND PROBLEM PLAYS – WOMEN    171

CX = Major (building)
ST = This moment could seal the deal of love between us. (Careful)

**AR (Lover)** [Hard to seem won; but I was won, my lord,
With the first glance that ever—**PG (I Close) QA (Apologetically)**
pardon me—
If I confess much, you will play the tyrant.
**PG (I Penetrate) QA (Controllingly)** I love you now; but not, till
now, so much
But I might master it. **PG (I Open) QA (Revealingly)** In faith, I lie:
My thoughts were like unbridled children, grown
Too headstrong for their mother. **QA (Exclamatorily)** See, we
fools!
**PG (I Close) QA (Chidingly-herself)** Why have I blabb'd? Who
shall be true to us,
When we are so unsecret to ourselves?
**PG (I Open) QA (Admittedly)** But, though I loved you well, I woo'd
you not;
And yet, good faith, I wish'd myself a man,
Or that we women had men's privilege
Of speaking first. **PG (I Close) QA (Pleadingly)** Sweet, bid me hold
my tongue,
For in this rapture I shall surely speak
The thing I shall repent. **PG (I Open) QA (Accusatorily)** See, see,
your silence,
Cunning in dumbness, from my weakness draws
My very soul of counsel—**QA (Laughingly)** stop my mouth!] *End
AF 1*

**Note: In this one you really have to understand the culture of the
men and women of Troy. Men of Troy were fierce warriors and their
demeanor around women was that of ruler—although women were
well respected in their place. Women, to counter this demeanor,
always played sort of hard to get. Here, Cressida is revealing
perhaps too much according to the culture. Yet, she can't help it as
both she and Troilus are eager to get on with it. Invest especially in
the PG's to capture the wonderful back and forth she is inwardly
experiencing.**

# THE PROBLEM PLAYS-MEN

## One

*Measure for Measure*
Act III, sc. i

Claudio—AR—Victim, Child Eternal, Lover

## MONOLOGUE

### *AF 1*

PG/AC = I Embrace/I Guilt
QA = Sorrowfully
BP = The Plea
OB = I want to live.
AM = Fear
OS = Isabella may not want to give up her virginity.
CX = Major (building)
ST = Life or Death


**AR (Victim)** [Ay, but to die, and go we know not where;
To lie in cold obstruction and to rot;
**QA (Tearfully)** This sensible warm motion to become
A kneaded clod; and the delighted spirit
To bathe in fiery floods, or to reside
In thrilling region of thick-ribbed ice;
**QA (Chillingly)** To be imprison'd in the viewless winds,
And blown with restless violence round about
The pendent world; **QA (Painfully)** or to be worse than worst
Of those that lawless and incertain thought
Imagine howling: 'tis too horrible.
**QA (Profoundly)** The weariest and most loathed worldly life
That age, ache, penury and imprisonment
Can lay on nature is a paradise
To what we fear of death.
[*Isabella—'Alas, alas.'*]
**QA (Beggingly)** Sweet sister, let me live:

THE ROMANCES AND PROBLEM PLAYS – WOMEN    173

What sin you do to save a brother's life,
Nature dispenses with the deed so far
That it becomes a virtue.] *End AF 1*

**Note: Some scholars have compared this speech to Hamlet's 'To be, or not to be.' I don't think so—at least in my interpretation of it. Hamlet is resolving himself to an early expiration. Claudio isn't. I think it is stronger for Claudio to convince Isabella to save his life by any means he can. It's just that he chooses different Actions and QA's to do so. Claudio wants to live to see his baby born and marry his fiancé.**

**End Chapter Six**

Other speeches to consider from the Problem Plays (Index of First Lines)

1. *Measure for Measure*
   Act III, sc. i
   Duke Vencentio—'Be absolute for death; either death or life. . . '

2. *Troilus and Cressida*
   Act I, sc. iii
   Ulysses—'The great Achilles, whom opinion crowns. . . '

# Appendix I

# EXERCISES-CONTRIBUTED BY COLLEAGUES AND TEACHERS OF THE GREAT LAKES MICHAEL CHEKHOV CONSORTIUM

## 1. Imaginary Body Exercise

### *Created and Contributed by Catherine Albers*

The inspiration for this exercise comes from Chapter 6 in Michael Chekhov's *To the Actor*. In describing an imaginary body, he writes, 'You clothe yourself, as it were, with this body; you put it on like a garment.' Over the years, as I've developed it, this exercise has grown. Many students have enlarged and deepened it. But the basic exercise remains the same. Side coaching is essential to this exercise, reminding the students of the Four Brothers—ease, form, beauty, and the whole—and guiding them to activate their actor's ideal center, their imaginations, and the things that they not only know about the character from the script but also what they intuit about the character. What follows is the basic structure of the exercise:

Lie down on the floor, and close your eyes. We begin this exercise by erasing your body. We begin by starting at your feet and moving upward. Imagine a large eraser that begins with one foot. It isn't painful, but rather nice, to slowly let go of all pressure and stress and simply erase your body. The eraser moves slowly, one appendage at a time, erasing each foot, each shin and thigh, each knee, etc. all the way up. This is an exercise in imagination and a commitment to the power of this work, as you eventually will erase your own head. Go slowly and erase the entire body and work with ease.

Now begin to imagine your character in minute detail. Begin at the head and work down, imagining every aspect of the body, including eye color, color of the hair and the style, shape of the ears and the nose

APPENDIX I CONTRIBUTED EXERCISES175

and the mouth, the chin, the neck and so on, down the entire length of the body. Imagine the foot and that shape, the toes and their length, etc. Every aspect is important, as this body will become yours. Ask your character questions about their Actions and what they do. And what brings them pleasure. Listen carefully to what they tell you. Store this information away as it will help in the next part of the exercise.

Once this is complete, sit up and open your eyes. 'See' a pile of clay in front of you. Interact with the clay, getting used to the feel of it and how it can be manipulated. Enjoy the sensation of the damp and pliable material in your hands. Allow ease to spread throughout your bodies, and begin, as a sculptor begins, to form the feet of the character, always allowing the character to tell you what they want to look like, how they want to be formed.

As you complete both feet, then slowly move up the body, shaping and molding the clay into the body of the character, moving around the clay to make the sides and the back of the body as fully formed as the front. Every detail is important. Take your time, and allow your imagination and your character to guide you.

When you reach the head of the character, shape these most intimate details, noting exactly how your character looks out at the world. When all aspects of the head are finished, walk around the character body and make sure it is complete. Touch it if you like, to feel the warmth, to understand the length of the arms, how the hands are formed. Standing in front of the character body, touch the feeling center. Let your light enter theirs. Move to the back of the body, facing the back of the character and begin the process of 'stepping in.' You may begin with a hand to feel what this other body is like or you may step in with one foot and then the other to fully enter. When ready, step totally in and put the body on as if you are putting on new clothes. Once you are fully 'in,' take a few minutes to understand the differences in this body.

What does it feel like to see with their eyes, to lift their hand, to simply breathe in and out? When you are ready, move about the space, experiencing the way this body walks, sits, and interacts with objects in the space. Now step out of the body, and into your own body. What is the difference now? Now step back in. And back out. Identify the trigger for your body to become the character body. Step in and out a few more times until that trigger is realized. Then step out completely and spy-back and note in your journals what was experienced.

# 2. Additional Exercise for Qualities of Movement

*The Seed Journey Exercise, Created and Contributed by Eva Gil*

'Consider your movements as little pieces of art.'

—Michael Chekhov

**Note: Qualities of Movement is not included in the 'formula' of the monologues. After you read and rehearse QoM in *To the Actor*, give this exercise a try. It is lovingly evolved from the original and will help elevate your physical being. Consider that each Artistic Frame may by a different QoM experiment. —M. Monday**

In Chapter 1 of *To the Actor*, Michael Chekhov presents exercises for the actor to discover Qualities of Movement, he named Molding, Flowing, Flying, and Radiating. As always, we are interested in what internal sensations are generated by these movements.

Find a spot in the room where you have space to work and curl up in a fetal position on the floor. Working with your eyes open, connect with your breath and allow ease to flow in your body with each inhale and exhale. Now, imagine that you are surrounded by warm, comforting soil. It is above you, below you, it cradles and supports you. Imagine you are a tiny seed underground. Slowly you begin to open up from your curled position. Maybe a finger or a wrist begins to move through the resistance of the soil, towards the source of the warmth above you. Maybe then the whole arm, the neck, and upwards you go, your whole body starts to move through the soil. There is resistance all around you; each movement has a beginning, middle, and end as you mold your way through the soil. If you looked back you could see the tunnel, the impressions you are leaving behind you as you mold your way through the soil, towards the source of the heat, which is drawing you upwards.

Suddenly, you are feeling less resistance and you have broken through the soil. What does the air feel like, surrounding you? How does it feel to be rooted in the soil? Allow yourself to discover a feeling of ease in the air, in the sun, while feeling securely rooted to the earth. You are able to move and sway in the gentle breeze, allowing

# APPENDIX I CONTRIBUTED EXERCISES 177

a flowing motion to emerge. Your roots (feet) are stationary, but the rest of your body flows; it is a continuous movement in the soft breeze. Flow with your arms, with your torso, with your neck, with your knees. As Chekhov says, 'Let them ebb and flow like big waves . . . imagine the air around you as a surface of water which supports you and over which your movements lightly skim.'

You continue to grow upwards, feeling that air around you, still rooted in the earth, but now imagine that there is a sudden, quick expansion of your petals (arms) and an opening of a bud into a blossom; radiate that openness and expansion. Open and expand as much as you are able to, and when you have reached the peak of your blossom expanding, radiate further into the space that feeling of openness and expansion. Chekhov instructs us in radiating, 'to go out and beyond the boundary of our body.' Find joy in that feeling of expansiveness and radiation.

Then suddenly a gust of wind shakes your blossom free from the stem and roots and you are whisked into the wind. Freed from your roots you are flying around the space quickly, one direction then another, then another, at the whim each gust of wind. Chekhov writes, 'Your desire must be to overcome the weight of your body, to fight the law of gravity.' Perhaps there are pauses as you soar for a moment, only to be taken again in another direction, then another.

The wind begins to die down and you fall slowly to the earth. You feel the soil beneath you; it is warm and comforting. Slowly soil begins to cover you up; gradually, you are blanketed by it: soft, warm, and reassuring. The strength of the sun begins to dim as you are covered up and surrounded by the soil. Slowly, contract your body back into a ball in a fetal position. Find comfort in the soil surrounding you, the stillness. To end the exercise, ask the participants to inhale and exhale together, three times, finding a group breath/rhythm.

Have them sit up and lead a spy-back on what they discovered about Qualities of Movement, their imaginative work and ability to find ease in the exploration. Possible spy-back questions could be: what did they discover when they were molding their way through the soil and felt resistance? What sensations developed when they were flowing in the gentle breeze? When they were whisked into the wind and flying around, what sensations arose? What sensations developed when they expanded and radiated as the blossom? When they contracted back into the ball at the end?

178 APPENDIX I CONTRIBUTED EXERCISES

**Notes: Allow ample time between the prompts for exploration and discovery; give them enough time to clock each QoM for themselves. Additionally, you may want to experiment with adding music, without lyrics, that exudes each Quality of Movement, but it works nicely either way.**

## 3. Additional Exercise for Psychological Gesture

### *Created and Contributed by Jennifer Tuttle*

Imagine a line on the ground, your own personal threshold. It can be anything you want it to be—a line drawn in chalk, a sting, a patch of grass—you don't have to look at it, but you can if you wish.

On this side of the threshold is the mundane. Your Lower Self. The you who walked in here with your literal and figurative baggage, your worries, your checklist of tasks. On the other side of the threshold, what's waiting for you is the sacred space, the creative space, your Higher Self, your Higher Ego.

Scan your body, breathe to any place you feel tension and let it go. Take stock of how you are feeling emotionally, mentally, physically— acknowledge where you are now in this moment, without judgment. Allow your mouth to open a bit; if you're tongue is pressed up against the roof of your mouth, let it relax—be permeable. Take in the space.

Warm up your hands by rubbing them together vigorously and place them on your Actor's Ideal Center (AIC). Your AIC is your emotional, feeling, heart center, which is the center of the Higher Ego, the place of origination for our Higher Self. Imagine there's a sun glowing in your AIC, warming it up. Can you feel it wanting to cross the threshold? Wanting to enter the sacred, creative space? Wanting to move from your Lower Self to your Higher Self and engage the Higher Ego? When you feel the AIC pulling you, irresistibly, I want you to follow that creative impulse and cross the threshold into your Higher Self and take a walk in the sacred, creative space.

Begin to walk through the space with an inward focus. Let any thoughts about what happened before you got here, or what you need to do tonight, or your physical state go—acknowledge them, but know that there will be time for them later. Be here now, in the moment. Feel your feet on the floor, feel your breath supporting you, find the tempo that you want to be walking in right now.

# APPENDIX I CONTRIBUTED EXERCISES          179

There are six directions in which a body can move in space. Right now you are walking forward. But I'd like to open up the others for you, one by one. These are options, not commands. As you feel the impulse to move in your AIC, in addition to moving forward, you may also move up. What are all the different ways your body can move up? Explore this as you feel the impulse in your Actor's Ideal Center.

Another option open to you is left, and by this, I don't mean, turn to the left and walk forward—I mean move your whole body to the left. How many ways is this possible? How does this feel—what are the sensations that arise in you when you do so? What goes up must also go down—that is another option open to you, when you feel the desire to do so. To balance out the left, you have the option to move your entire body to the right. Again, check in with your self—what sensations arise when you move your body in this direction.

I have one more direction to open up to you, but before I do, I want you to focus on your backspace, which encompasses the entire backside of your body and the space behind it. Imagine that the sun that's in your AIC is expanding and can send rays of radiant energy pouring out of your entire back body, into the space, and even through the walls and beyond—this is called radiating. Once you've radiated out and into your backspace, then you can move backward—with the caveat that you never move faster in this direction than your backspace can radiate and sense what's behind it, so as not to hurt yourself. Only when you feel your backspace is alive and radiant, can you explore backwards.

Finally, take a few minutes to let yourself explore all six directions, as your impulses desire. Many of these directions are combinable—for example, I'm sure you could move up and forward at the same time! Or down and to the left! Let your body explore these. Take stock of the sensations and feelings that you associate with these six directions one more time, so that the essence of them is alive in your instrument.

Come to stillness, and then go get your text: your sonnet, soliloquy, or monologue. Begin to read your text out loud, thought by thought and physically move in one or more of the six directions with each thought—don't THINK about which direction you should move—let your Actor's Ideal Center move you in the direction that the thought wants your body to move in.

Once you've walked all the thoughts of your text, come to stillness, and this time, when you read each thought aloud, note which direction, or directions are ignited in your AIC. For example: If your first

180    APPENDIX I CONTRIBUTED EXERCISES

thought is 'O for a muse of fire' you might feel a tug in your AIC to move up and forward. Let those directions be a guide to what PG you would choose to apply to that piece of text, using Artistic Frame. In this case, the Lift PG moves up and forward. From your zero point, Imagine, DO and radiate the Psychological Gesture of Lift. At the sweet spot of the radiation, speak the thought 'O for a muse of fire'—does this engage your AIC? If so, move on to the next thought! If not, try other PGs with Artistic Frame that move either forward or up to see if they ignite your text. You can score your entire speech this way.

Once you've scored your text with Psychological Gesture, using the Artistic Frame of Imagine, DO, Radiate, you can drop the form of the PG, but retain the essence of it in your Actor's Ideal Center. Speak the speech aloud, let your body move with the essence of the gesture alive in your instrument. Expand it! This should make the text come alive in the moment, in the space and be fully psychophysically realized.

### *Directions in Which the Psychological Gestures Move*

Open—forward
Close—down
Smash—down and forward
Tear—down, left/right
Push—forward
Pull—back
Lift—up and forward
Throw—forward and up
Penetrate—forward and back
Embrace—left/right and forward
Twist—down and either left/right

## 4. In-Class/Rehearsal Exercise

### *Subjective/Objective Atmosphere Created and Contributed by Nicole Perrone*

'Just as in everyday life one speaks, moves, and acts differently when surrounded by different atmospheres, so on the stage

# APPENDIX I CONTRIBUTED EXERCISES 181

the actor will realize that the Atmosphere urges him to new nuances in his speech, movements, actions and feelings.'
—Michael Chekhov, *On the Technique of Acting*

This exploration is inspired by the chapter entitled, 'The Auditioning Event' in the book *Auditioning* by Joanna Merlin.

As a class or ensemble, move about the space taking in all that you perceive—not only what you see but also the smells, the sounds, the light in the space—natural or artificial, and the presence of your classmates. Attempt to do this without imposing any personal feelings onto the exercise, rather just take in what is there. After a few moments, pause and think of a word that summarizes the current atmosphere of the space you're exploring. Pause now and take several deep cleansing breaths. Resume walking the space and now imagine that you are waiting in the lobby or waiting room for an audition. As you move about the space, notice how your breathing has changed in accordance with this new atmosphere. As you notice an object in the space—a chair, a bag, etc., interact with it allowing your interaction to be colored by the atmosphere. Notice the other actors in the space and allow the atmosphere to inform your (silent) interactions with them as well. After a few moments, define the atmosphere you have been imagining in the space by naming it or 'baptizing' it. Pause again and take several deep cleansing breaths. Resume walking the space one last time and now imagine a place in which you feel completely at ease. Challenge yourself to go beyond a general choice such as 'my house' and to think of a specific place in your house in which you feel most at ease: the armchair by the fireplace, in bed on a rainy day, etc. What other elements contribute to this feeling of ease—the smells, sounds, and light in your 'happy place?' As you continue to move about the room, interact with an object or piece of furniture in the space, allowing it to provide comfort to you and bolster your feelings of ease. Once you've spent a few moments exploring, then think of a word to summarize the atmosphere you're imagining. Pause and take several deep cleansing breaths. At this point, take a few moments for spy-back with your ensemble. Did you feel different in each atmosphere? How? Did you notice your breath changing? Your tempo? Share the word(s) you used to name each atmosphere. Remember that the first atmosphere you explored was the atmosphere already present in the room: the

182     APPENDIX I CONTRIBUTED EXERCISES

*objective* atmosphere. Within the *objective* atmosphere of this classroom or rehearsal space, you were then able to cultivate two distinct *subjective* atmospheres solely through your use of your imagination.

Now choose three volunteers from among your group. Imagine that your classroom is an audition waiting room and set up three chairs in a row in the center. Two of the volunteers will sit on the two outside chairs leaving one open in the middle for the third volunteer who will go into the hall to prepare. In the hall, this actor will take a few moments to reconnect to that atmosphere of ease, ('peace,' 'warmth,' or 'joy'—whatever they named it) in the previous exercise. They will bring that atmosphere into the audition room with them whenever they are ready and take a seat in the center chair. They will not speak during the exercise—just wait for their name to be called.

While they are in the hall preparing, the remaining actors in the ensemble will adopt a contrary audition room atmosphere such as frenetic, unfocused, hostile, competitive, etc. Decide together as a group exactly what word you will use to define it. When the hallway actor enters the two actors seated in the outside chairs, as well as all other actors observing silently adopt this new atmosphere thereby transforming the objective atmosphere of the classroom or rehearsal space. When the actor enters from the hall, we have the experience of observing the collision of these two conflicting atmospheres. Your teacher or director will stop the exercise at the point that one of the atmospheres begins to 'win out' over the other. Now spy-back. Was the actor who attempted to embody a subjective atmosphere of ease able to maintain that within the objective atmosphere created by the ensemble? How could you tell that one atmosphere was winning out over the other?

## 5. Sensations-Rising, Balancing, Falling

### *Contributed by Christopher M. Bohan*

Sensations is a psycho-physical exercise that explores three distinct physical movements (Rising, Falling, Balancing) and the corresponding psycho-physical sensation received from each movement. Sensations can be used to score a frame, to build an imaginary body, but they are ideally used in response to outside stimuli. If a character receives good news, they may experience the Sensation of Rising, or

APPENDIX I CONTRIBUTED EXERCISES          183

if a character receives distressing news, they may experience the Sensation of Falling. And, uncertain news may bring on the Sensation of Balancing.

In the Michael Chekhov Technique, we have the Big R (Radiating) in the Qualities of Movement (Radiating, Molding, Flowing, Flying), and the little 'r' in how we radiate in six directions (Staccato, Legato). And, we have the Big S for Sensations (Rising, Falling, Balancing) and the little 's' for sensations received in our Actors Ideal Center (AIC) when we execute Psychological Gestures, work with the Qualities of Movement, or exercise with any of the other aspects of the psychophysical technique.

### *EXERCISE #1: RISING*

Each participant should find a sturdy chair and sit at the edge, feet flat on the floor. Engage the Actors Ideal Center and allow for a feeling of ease. With a feeling of ease, ACTOR will leap into the air and land on two feet in front of the chair. Even when the physical body has come to a static position, the Life-Body should continue Rising. Check in with AIC: what sensation are you receiving from Rising? Radiate (small r) that sensation in six directions. Repeat 3x.

### *EXERCISE #2: FALLING*

Actor sits on edge of chair, feet flat on the floor. Place hands alongside hips and press palms firmly into chair raising self-off the chair by one or two inches. Engage the Actors Ideal Center and allow for a feeling of ease. Release hands from chair, falling into chair. Even when physical body comes to stop, allow Life-Body to continue Falling. Check in with AIC. What is the sensation received from Falling? Radiate that sensation in six directions. Repeat 3x.

### *EXERCISE #3: BALANCING*

Actor stands in space. Engage the Actors Ideal Center and allow for a feeling of ease. Take one foot off the floor and begin Balancing. The goal is not to find your balance, but rather to experience the sensation of Balancing. If you have a good sense of balance, work with eyes

184    APPENDIX I CONTRIBUTED EXERCISES

closed, or work with a partner by holding one hand and work to keep the other person off balance. Then, bring the physical body to a static position while allowing the Life-Body to continue Balancing. Check in with AIC. What is the sensation received from Balancing? Radiate that sensation in six directions. Repeat 3x.

*EXERCISE #4: THE SENSATIONS AND THE ARTISTIC FRAME*

Actor begins by allowing a Feeling if Ease to enter the AIC. Actor will *Fantasize* their Life-Body walking a path in the room and stopping at a specific point in the room. Actor will *Do* the path the Life-Body took and, when stopped, will *Radiate* the sensation received from walking the path in six directions.

Go back to your starting point.

Actor will Fantasize their Life-Body walking the same path in the room, stopping at 1 point along the path, then continuing to the original stopping point creating an Artistic Frame (Beginning, Middle, End). Actor will DO the path, stopping at the middle for a moment, then continue to the End.

Go back to the starting point.

Actor will stand at the Beginning of the path and endow the space with one of the Sensations (Rising, Falling, Balancing), then continue on the path endowing each point (Middle and End) with each of the remaining Sensations. Once each part of the Artistic Frame has been endowed, go back to the starting point.

Then, the actor will complete the path while engaging the Sensations:

Actor stands at Beginning, allowing a Feeling of Ease to enter the AIC.

Actor engages the Sensation of Rising and radiates the sensation as they move to the Middle.

At the middle, the Actor engages the sensation of Balancing and radiates the sensation of Balancing as they walk toward the end. At the End, the Actor engages the sensation of Falling and radiates that sensation in six directions, completing the Artistic Frame.

## Application of Sensations to Monologue Work

Traditionally, an actor will score their monologue with Actions, or if using the Michael Chekhov Technique, they may score their monologue

APPENDIX I CONTRIBUTED EXERCISES          185

using Psychological Gestures or the Qualities of Movement. Scoring a monologue with Sensations is a simple process and can help the actor discover the psycho-physical response their character experiences when facing obstacles.

Similar to Exercise #4, the actor will break their monologue down into three Artistic Frames: Beginning, Middle, and End. Then, the Actor will endow each individual Frame with a Sensation. Using the given circumstances as their guide, the actor will endow the frame with the Sensation they believe the character is experiencing at the time. For the Beginning frame, it is helpful to use Joanna Merlin's Pre-Beat to help establish the first Sensation, as well as adding a Post-Beat at the end to engage the Sensation that results from getting their objective or failing.

For Example:

**Pre Beat: Character is about to propose***

Sensation: Balancing
Exercise: Actor stands on one foot before they speak

**Beginning Artistic Frame: Character gets down on one knee**

Sensation: Rising
Exercise: Actor will jump into the air and radiate the sensation of Rising while speaking the frame. (Even though the character is literally on one knee, the Sensation they are experiencing in the AIC is Rising!)

**Middle Artistic Frame: other character backed up**

Sensation: Balancing
Exercise: Actor will stand on one foot and radiate the Sensation of Balancing while speaking the frame.

**End Artistic Frame: Other character has taken the ring**

Sensation: Rising
Exercise: Actor will jump into the air and radiate the Sensation of Rising while speaking the frame.

186 APPENDIX I CONTRIBUTED EXERCISES

**Post-Beat: Other character said 'no' and returned ring**

Sensation: Falling

Exercise: Actor will fall into a chair and radiate the Sensation of
Falling as the other character leaves.

*A note on Polarity:* I would strongly urge you to experiment with using
the Polar Sensation when working monologues, especially early in the
process. It may be the easy (correct, even) choice to engage the Sensation of Balancing when about to propose, but allow yourself to explore
what happens with Falling, or Rising before you begin the monologue.
Remember, these are tools used to explore character. The Michael
Chekhov Technique is a means to an end, not the end in and of itself.

## 6. The Life-Body

### *Contributed by Lionel Walsh*

Michael Chekhov advises us to imagine 'that your arms and legs originate
from' an 'imaginary center as source of inner activity and *power* within
your body' (Chekhov, 2002) p 7. He instructs us to send this power not
only throughout the body, but to 'let the power which flows from the
imaginary center within your chest and leads you through the space *precede*
the movement itself' and to let that power 'flow and radiate beyond . . .
the boundaries of your body and into the space around you.' Chekhov
teacher, Lenard Petit, coined the term Life-Body to identify this energy.
Petit says that the using the image of the Life-Body 'gives form to the
energy' to which Chekhov refers in *To the Actor.* (Petit, 2010) pp. 32–33.

This exercise is adapted from Michael Chekhov and Lenard Petit.

Stand in the space with your feet in parallel position under your hips
and let your breath drop in, using your diaphragm to support deep
breathing.

Feel your feet on the floor and allow your breath to exhale through
your mouth so you jaw in released.

Raise your arm toward the ceiling and then, after a moment, lower
it. Note that you can feel your arm raising and lowering. Repeat with
your other arm. Do this a few times until you have a strong physical
feeling of your arm moving in space.

APPENDIX I CONTRIBUTED EXERCISES          187

Now, imagine that inside your arm is another arm, the same size and shape as your physical arm. It is connected to your Feeling Centre in the middle of your chest and any movement your energy arm does begins in your Feeling Centre.

Now, raise your energy arm towards the ceiling, beginning the movement in your heart center, sending energy and light into the space, and allow your physical arm to follow it.

Once your physical movement stops, keep sending your energy arm beyond the boundaries of your physical arm, imagining it going up to the ceiling, through it and into space beyond. Keep radiating the light and energy of your Life-Body arm beyond your body until you feel it beginning to wane. Then send your Life-Body arm back down to your side, allowing your physical arm to follow it. Continue the flow of energy and light down to the floor, beneath it, imagining that it flows to the center of the earth.

Note that you should feel your energy body moving just as you do your physical body. It is not important to see it.

Continue this process, moving your arms in the six directions—up, down, right, left, forward, and back. Experiment with a lunge forward, beginning the movement of your leg with your Life-Body in your Feeling Centre, following with your physical leg, and imagining the energy and light radiating to the center of the earth.

Now, imagine a full energy body inside your physical body and send it out ahead of your physical body, for a walk through the space. Continue your walk sending your Life-Body, following it with your physical body.

Note that employing your Life-Body gives you the impulse to move through the space and gives you the sense of being bigger than you are in your everyday life. It also gives you a feeling of power that you can use on stage to heighten your presence with your acting partners and with the audience.

After a while, allow your physical body to come to a stop but keep radiating your Life-Body forward, allowing the energy to stream out of you. Feel the pull of your energy body, giving you the impulse to follow it. When the impulse to walk is strong, follow it.

Repeat this several times. Then, when your physical body stops, keep sending out your Life-Body, then pull it almost back inside your physical body, and then send it out again. Keep flexing this Life-Body muscle

188 APPENDIX I CONTRIBUTED EXERCISES

in this manner until the impulse to follow it physically is so strong that you cannot resist following it. Repeat a few times.

If you are working in a group, as you walk through the space, radiate your Life-Body to the others in the space, receiving their Life-Bodies as you pass them. Again, focus on feeling your Life-Body flowing out of you and on feeling your colleagues' Life-Bodies as you receive them.

Eventually, allow your physical body to come to a stop, and continue to radiate your Life-Body into the space. When you feel the energy beginning to wane, pull your Life-Body back in and step away.

### INCORPORATING TEXT

It is when the actor incorporates the effects of the exercise into the monologue, scene, or entire play that inspiration occurs. To do so requires concentration to sustain the actor's imagination, which in this case supports the incorporation of the Life-Body into the text.

To prepare, choose and memorize a monologue. This can be a monologue that you have worked on previously or one that is new to you. Next, determine a threshold around the perimeter of your rehearsal space. Inside this threshold is the playing space or 'stage' and outside of it is the 'wings.'

### PART ONE

Choose a phrase from your monologue. This can be the opening line, the climax of the monologue, or a phrase that appeals to your creative imagination.

Stand in the wings and imagine your Life-Body. Feel it concentrated in your Feeling Centre, radiating from there throughout your whole physical body. Next, fantasize your Life-Body crossing the threshold to a specific spot on the 'stage.' Then, beginning the radiation from your Feeling Centre, send your Life-Body across the threshold to the spot on the stage that you have chosen, following it with your physical body. Once you have hit your mark, continue to radiate and rehearse the phrase you have chosen. Sustain the radiation and send your Life-Body into the wings, making an exit, and following it with your physical body. Repeat this several times until you are able to sustain the incorporation of your Life-Body from your entrance to your exit.

APPENDIX I CONTRIBUTED EXERCISES 189

*PART TWO*

Using the first beat of your monologue, follow the same process as in Part One. Repeat several times until you are able to sustain the incorporation of your Life-Body from entrance to exit. Repeat this process with each successive beat of your monologue until you have rehearsed the entire piece by one beat at a time.

*PART THREE*

Then, repeat the process, incorporating Life-Body into an entrance, rehearsal of the monologue in its entirety, and an exit. Repeat several times until you can sustain the incorporation of the Life-Body into the rehearsal from entrance to exit.

*WORKING WITH A PARTNER*

Choose a partner and decide who is A and who is B. In this exercise you and your partner will radiate your Life-Bodies to one another. Stand facing your partner, about seven feet apart. Partner A, beginning the movement in your Feeling Centre, activate your Life-Body and send it to Partner B. Partner B, place yourself in a receptive mode and when you feel Partner A's Life-Body contact you, raise your arm. Now switch roles. Repeat a few times until both partners feel they are able to send their Life-Body and receive that of their partner. Then, engage in an exchange of Life-Bodies in a continuous flow without raising your arm to indicate you have received your partner's Life-Body. Instead, as you radiate your Life-Body to your partner, receive your partner as you radiate so that you know by their reaction when your Life-Body has been received. Let the exchange be a constant flow of radiating and receiving between you. Do this for one or two minutes.

Next, following the process in the paragraph above, Partner A will begin by radiating their Life-Body to Partner B. When you see that Partner B has received your Life-Body begin rehearsing your monologue. Partner B receive Partner A moment-to-moment, allowing yourself to radiate your reaction back to Partner A. At the end of the monologue, both partners should sustain the final moment for a few seconds before stepping away. Then reverse roles and repeat.

190    APPENDIX I CONTRIBUTED EXERCISES

### *FANTASTIC ACTION*[1]

Just as you can simply send your Life-Body to a point on the stage or to your acting partner, you can also execute a Fantastic Action with your Life-Body that supports your physical and psychological Actions. These Fantastic Actions can be ones that are possible in life, such as gently touching your partner's cheek, or ones that are not literally possible, such as brushing the cobwebs out of your partner's brain. These Fantastic Actions may be done at a specified moment in your monologue or may be sustained throughout. Choose Fantastic Actions that make sense for the circumstances of your monologue and the physical/psychological Action you have chosen. Ask yourself, 'If I could, what would I do to him or her?' These Fantastic Actions are in our lexicon: 'You broke my heart.' 'You are tearing me to pieces.' 'I'm going to poke your eyes out!' 'I'm going to touch your heart.' You can also do things such as viscously break your partner's heart, gently clear the cobwebs out of her head, cruelly disembowel him, tickle her lightly, slowly tear the skin off his face, or pinch her playfully. Note the use of a Quality in these descriptions. Of course, you can make up your own as they suit your given circumstances and the physical/psychological Action you have chosen. Now you are ready to experiment with this exercise.

Prepare as you did above, and then radiate your Life-Body towards your partner, beginning the rehearsal of your text once you see that your partner has received your Life-Body. Then, as you speak the text, support your Action by adding your Fantastic Action at the appropriate moment or moments during the monologue. There is no need to 'perform' your monologue, or rehearse it at a normal pace. Allow yourself to take your time, relishing in the execution of your Fantastic Action as you speak your text. Pause when you feel the need. You should feel a deeper sense of purpose and power, as well as an added dimension to your Action. Note that it is not important that your partner know what your Fantastic Action is, or even that you are doing one. What is important is the effect on your partner as you do the Fantastic Action and what it makes him do in response. In fact, I advise that you do not reveal your Fantastic Action to your partner so that it keeps the power of the unknown. Remember to receive that response and allow it to affect you as you work your way through the monologue. Repeat your rehearsal a number of times, each time increasing your pace a little, until you are rehearsing it at a pace that you feel is right for the piece.

APPENDIX I CONTRIBUTED EXERCISES 191

Eventually, you will find that you no longer need to do the Fantastic Action, that the effects of doing it have been incorporated into the text. Then reverse roles and repeat.

## 7. The Psychological Gestures (Video)

*Contributed by Jamie Koeth and Leah Smith*

www.routledge.com/9780367349707

## Note

1  This exercise was developed in the Inspired Acting Lab at the University of Windsor with the support of the Outstanding Scholars and Ignite Work Study Programs.

# Appendix II

# PRACTICE MONOLOGUES FOR IDENTIFYING THE SCORE

You will find here monologues in which I have inserted places for you to develop the score. Keep in mind that these choices are mine and therefore not ideal for your end purposes. Still, the exercise of doing the work where I suggest an Action or Quality of Action is a good forward step to ultimately finding the full score for yourself.

## COMEDIES-MEN

### One

*As You Like It*
Act II, sc. vii

Jacques—AR—Actor, Child Orphan, Addict, Muse, Poet, Scholar

### *AF 1*

PG/AC =
QA =
BP =
OB =
AM =
OS =
CX =
ST =

**AR (**           **)** [A fool, a fool! I met a fool i' the forest,
A motley fool; a miserable world!

# APPENDIX II MONOLOGUES FOR IDENTIFYING 193

**QA** (            ) As I do live by food, I met a fool
Who laid him down and bask'd him in the sun,
And rail'd on Lady Fortune in good terms,
In good set terms **PG** (            ) **QA** (            ) and yet a
    motley fool.
**QA** (            ) 'Good morrow, fool,' quoth I. **PG** (            )
    **QA** (            ) 'No, sir,' quoth he,
'Call me not fool till heaven hath sent me fortune:'
**PG** (            ) **QA** (            ) And then he drew a dial from
    his poke,
And, looking on it with lack-lustre eye,
Says very wisely, **PG** (            ) **QA** (            ) 'It is ten o'clock:
Thus we may see,' quoth he, 'how the world wags;
'Tis but an hour ago since it was nine,
And after one hour more 'twill be eleven;
And so, from hour to hour, we ripe and ripe,
And then, from hour to hour, we rot and rot;
And thereby hangs a tale.' **PG** (            ) **QA** (            ) When
    I did hear
The motley fool thus moral on the time,
My lungs began to crow like chanticleer,
That fools should be so deep-contemplative,
And I did laugh sans intermission
An hour by his dial. **PG** (            ) **QA** (            ) O noble fool!
A worthy fool! Motley's the only wear.] *End AF 1*

## Two

*Much Ado About Nothing*
Act II, sc. iii

Benedick—AR—Lover, Child Eternal, Poet, Liberator, Judge

### *AF 1*

PG/AC =
QA =
BP =
OB =

# 194 APPENDIX II MONOLOGUES FOR IDENTIFYING

AM =
OS =
CX =
ST =


**AR** ( ) [This can be no trick: the
conference was sadly borne. They have the truth of
this from Hero. They seem to pity the lady: it
seems her affections have their full bent. **PG** ( )
   **QA** ( ) Love me!
**QA** ( ) Why, it must be requited. **PG** ( )
   **QA** ( ) I hear how I am censured:
they say I will bear myself proudly, if I perceive
the love come from her; they say too that she will
rather die than give any sign of affection. **QA** ( ) I did
never think to marry. **PG** ( ) **QA** ( ) I must not
   seem proud: happy
are they that hear their detractions and can put
them to mending. **PG** ( ) **QA** ( ) They say the
   lady is fair; 'tis a
truth, I can bear them witness; **QA** ( ) and virtuous; 'tis
so, I cannot reprove it; **QA** ( ) and wise, **PG** ( )
   **QA** ( ) but for loving
me; by my troth, it is no addition to her wit, nor
no great argument of her folly, for I will be
horribly in love with her. **PG** ( ) **QA** ( ) I may
   chance have some
odd quirks and remnants of wit broken on me,
because I have railed so long against marriage: **QA** ( ) but
doth not the appetite alter? **PG** ( ) **QA** ( )
   A man loves the meat
in his youth that he cannot endure in his age.
**PG** ( ) **QA** ( ) Shall quips and sentences and
   these paper bullets of
the brain awe a man from the career of his humour?
**PG** ( ) **QA** ( ) No, the world must be peopled.
   **PG** ( ) **QA** ( )

# APPENDIX II MONOLOGUES FOR IDENTIFYING 195

When I said I would
die a bachelor, I did not think I should live till I
were married. **PG** (        ) **QA** (        ) Here comes Bea-
    trice. **PG** (        ) **QA** (        )
By this day!
She's a fair lady: I do spy some marks of love in her.] *End AF 1*

## COMEDIES-WOMEN

## One

*The Comedy of Errors*
Act II, sc. ii

Adriana—AR—Lover, Child Eternal, Poet

### *AF 1*

PG/AC =
QA =
BP =
OB =
AM =
OS =
CX =
ST =

**AR** (        ) [Ay, ay, Antipholus, look strange and frown:
Some other mistress hath thy sweet aspects;
I am not Adriana nor thy wife.
**PG** (        ) **QA** (        ) The time was once when thou
    unurged wouldst vow
That never words were music to thine ear,
That never object pleasing in thine eye,
That never touch well welcome to thy hand,
That never meat sweet-savor'd in thy taste,

196    APPENDIX II MONOLOGUES FOR IDENTIFYING

Unless I spake, or look'd, or touch'd, or carved to thee.
**PG (**              **) QA (**              **)** How comes it now, my husband,
       O, how comes it,
That thou art thus estranged from thyself?
**QA (**              **)** Thyself I call it, being strange to me,
That, undividable, incorporate,
Am better than thy dear self's better part.
**PG (**              **) QA (**              **)** Ah, do not tear away thyself
       from me!
**PG (**              **) QA (**              **)** For know, my love, as easy may-
       est thou fall
A drop of water in the breaking gulf,
And take unmingled that same drop again,
Without addition or diminishing,
As take from me thyself and not me too.
**PG (**              **) QA (**              **)** How dearly would it touch me
       to the quick,
Shouldst thou but hear I were licentious
And that this body, consecrate to thee,
By ruffian lust should be contaminate!
**PG (**              **) QA (**              **)** Wouldst thou not spit at me and
       spurn at me
And hurl the name of husband in my face
And tear the stain'd skin off my harlot-brow
And from my false hand cut the wedding-ring
And break it with a deep-divorcing vow?
**PG (**              **) QA (**              **)** I know thou canst; and therefore
       see thou do it.
**PG (**              **) QA (**              **)** I am possess'd with an adulter-
       ate blot;
My blood is mingled with the crime of lust:
For if we too be one and thou play false,
I do digest the poison of thy flesh,
Being strumpeted by thy contagion.
**PG (**              **) QA (**              **)** Keep then far league and truce
       with thy true bed;
I live unstain'd, thou undishonoured.] *End AF 1*

# APPENDIX II MONOLOGUES FOR IDENTIFYING 197

## Two

*A Midsummer Night's Dream*
Act III, sc. ii

Puck—AR—Fool, Child Magical, Slave, Rebel, Rescuer

### *AF 1*

PG/AC =
QA =
BP =
OB =
AM =
OS =
CX =
ST =

**AR** (   ) [My mistress with a monster is in love.
Near to her close and consecrated bower,
While she was in her dull and sleeping hour,
A crew of patches, rude mechanicals,
That work for bread upon Athenian stalls,
Were met together to rehearse a play
Intended for great Theseus' nuptial-day.
**QA** (   ) The shallowest thick-skin of that barren sort,
Who Pyramus presented, in their sport
Forsook his scene and enter'd in a brake
When I did him at this advantage take,
An ass's nole I fixed on his head.
**PG** (  ) **QA** (   ) Anon his Thisbe must be answered,
And forth my mimic comes. **QA** (   ) When they him spy,
**QA** (   ) As wild geese that the creeping fowler eye,
Or russet-pated choughs, many in sort,
Rising and cawing at the gun's report,
Sever themselves and madly sweep the sky,
So, at his sight, away his fellows fly;
And, at our stamp, here o'er and o'er one falls;

# 198     APPENDIX II MONOLOGUES FOR IDENTIFYING

He murder cries and help from Athens calls.
**PG** (          ) **QA** (               ) Their sense thus weak, lost with
    their fears thus strong,
Made senseless things begin to do them wrong;
For briers and thorns at their apparel snatch;
Some sleeves, some hats, from yielders all things catch.
**PG** (          ) **QA** (            ) I led them on in this distracted fear,
And left sweet Pyramus translated there:
When in that moment, so it came to pass,
Titania waked and straightway loved an ass.] *End AF 1*

# Appendix III

## COMPILATION OF NOTES PERTINENT TO ALL SPEECHES

1. Note: The larger the role the more AR's you'll find. The AR's arise depending on the given circumstances. Here you'll find nuances in Imaginary Body and Jewelry.
2. Be careful with the rhyming couplets. Use your operative words and you won't fall into a pattern of stressing all equally. Be sure to give varied weight to operative words.
3. Work hard on the changes of QA. They should be like 'springboards.' Each new quality should spring into a new thought with increased energy.

   You will have noticed that QA's can constantly change. That doesn't necessarily mean that your AC or OB needs to change. In fact, it is much simpler and more dynamic for the actor to look for QA changes in AF's. QA's are the territory of the actor and the actor only!
4. As this is the first soliloquy, I should reveal a strong belief I have about playing it and all other soliloquies. Obviously, there is no one on stage to play to. So, who is the character talking to and what could possibly be her objective? It is the audience. In most soliloquies the character is trying to solve a problem. In this speech Helena is musing on love and attempting to figure a way to win Demetrius. It is very active to use the audience as a literal scene partner. Rally the audience to your aid! Convince them to be on your side on your journey. What a journey it is. Invest in all of the wonderful QA changes and you'll have a blast—so will the audience.
5. Polarity (PL) is achieved by change in QA's and in the manner in which you build each speech.

6. Note: When you encounter an AX in the text it does not necessarily mean louder. Rather, it is an investment from the actor to heighten her or his subjective atmosphere. It is an inward commitment to the given circumstances. In our Technique it is an Expansion. Please see Appendix I for an explanation on Expansion–Contraction.

7. Note: PG changes are completely subjective as is all of the work in these scores. The score appears from the way I have acted them and then conducted painstaking spy-back on my work. In the end the work will be yours, and you can change AC, QA, and PG's as you discover your own journey in the speeches. There is something I would caution you on: don't overburden the text with change for change sake.

8. Note: We don't always need to state an AC other than the PG. In fact, the more you use this Technique the less you'll need to specify the AC beyond the PG.

9. As you begin to embody the Technique and eventually (after much repetition) begin to master it, you can incorporate more and more into each speech, scene, or even a single line or word. The Technique has many aspects. Take your time. Use one tool at a time, and then begin to layer.

10. Note: It's time to remind the reader/actor/teacher that these QA's and PG's have not come to me intellectually. They have occurred organically by Doing—on my feet. It is a good thing to try these choices as written. You'll find it to be a good exercise, but it will not be an organic process. Find your own choices—on your feet!

11. Note: The Elizabethans wholeheartedly believed in demonic spirits. You have to buy into this idea to make the stakes high and ground the speech in reality.

12. In longer speeches such as this it is important to remember that you can, when rehearsing, physically reinvest in the PG. You can always insert more PG's if you feel the need. I find it unnecessary to change the Action unless it is truly called for. QA changes most often suffice.

13. Chekhov suggested we see the objective completed before we begin our Actions. This is great advice. We have succeeded before we have begun.

14. Note: You can always, while rehearsing, reinvest in your PG. In fact, it is a good idea while finding, on your feet, how to build

the speech in volume, tempo, etc. Reinvestment in the PG also increases the will power—making your radiation stronger.

15. Note: When working with only one PG for the entire speech it is a good idea to build it with tempo and intensity. Sometimes we 'Squeeze' hard and then back off a bit. Nonetheless, we are always 'Squeezing.' You can always reinvest in the PG as you rehearse.

16. Note: As with any speech there is always interpretation. You may notice that this speech begins with the QA 'giddily' and ends with the QA 'bitterly.' I followed Chekhov's Laws of Composition using this concept of Polarity. This concept tells us that the beginning of the play, in this case speech, should transform itself into its opposite at the end. Just this one simple idea helps give the play, or speech, a simple way to create a dynamic Rhythmical Wave. It's a great idea to work on the beginning and then the ending and then proceed to the middle. Guiding your QA's in between the two will aid in creating a pathway that is vigorous and energetic. In your exploration always look for opposite QA's.

# INDEX

Aaron 115–116

AC *see* Action

Accents (AX): definition 1; in sonnets 16

Action (AC): definition 1; in sonnets 30–31

Actor's Ideal Center (AIC) 178–180, 183–184, 185

Adriana 195–196

AF *see* Artistic Frame

AIC *see* Actor's Ideal Center

Albers, Catherine 174

*All's Well That Ends Well* 167–169

AM *see* Atmosphere

Antony 105–106

*Antony and Cleopatra* 79–82, 96–98

AR *see* Archetype

Archetypal Gesture 6

Archetype (AR): definition 1–2; monologues 93; researching 157; in sonnets 31; in speeches 33

*Archetype Cards* (Myss) 2

Artistic Frame (AF): definition 2; exercises 180, 184–185; in sonnets 31

*As You Like It* 32, 33–40, 61–64, 192–193

Atmosphere (AM) 1, 2; *Antony and Cleopatra* 98; *Coriolanus* 100; definition 3; exercises 180–182; *Julius Caesar* 103, 106; *The Tempest* 166

audience: attitude to character 150; character knowledge 2; involvement in sonnets and soliloquies 23, 108, 141; and Rhythmical Wave 31, 141

*Auditioning* (Merlin) 181

auditions: character development 33; exercises 182; monologues 33, 87, 93, 122, 129, 133, 135, 139, 162, 164; soliloquies 77, 108; sonnets 7

AX *see* Accents

Balancing 182–186

Baptism (BP) 4

beats 185, 189

Benedick 71–73, 193–195

Berowne 64–66

Bishop of Carlisle 137–139

Bohan, Christopher M. 182

Bottom 70–71

BP *see* Baptism

breath 31, 44, 181

Brutus 104–105

# INDEX

Caliban 164–165

Calphurnia 87–88

Cassius 102–103

character: and Action 1; and archetypes 1–2, 5; Michael Chekhov Technique approach to 32–33; in Shakespeare's comedies 32; and Objective 5; Psychological Gesture 6

characterization: exercises 174–175; in sonnets 7, 9, 31

Chekhov, Michael: on atmosphere and archetypes 3; on climaxes 4; on flowing 177; on form 2; on imaginary center 186; on movements 176; on objective 2, 108; *On the Technique of Acting* 181; on Psychological Gesture 6; on radiating 177; *To the Actor* 4, 174, 176, 186; on transformation 5

Chorus (*Henry V*) 122–124, 147

Claudio 172–173

Cleopatra 79–82

Climaxes (CX): definition 4; monologues 88; soliloquies 77; in sonnets 31

comedies (Shakespeare): men 61–77, 192–195; women 32–61, 195–198

*Comedy of Errors, The* 40–42, 195–198

Composition 4; *see also* Laws of Composition

conflict 3

Coriolanus (character in *Coriolanus*) 99–100

*Coriolanus* 98–100

Cressida 170–171

cross gender casting 7

CX *see* Climaxes

*Cymbeline:* monologue 160–162; soliloquy 156–157

*Directing with the Michael Chekhov Technique* (Monday) 1

double entendres 80

Duchess of Gloucester 119–120

Duke Senior 61–62

Edmund 107–108

Eleanor 126–128

Emelia 93–94

emotion 2–3, 82, 106, 120, 131, 135, 144, 178

energy 4, 37, 45, 179, 186–188

Enobarbus 96–98

exercises: Archetype 33; Atmosphere 31, 180–182; character and characterization 174–175; Fantastic Action 190–191; Imaginary Body 32; Life-Body 186–191; monologues 184–186, 188–190, 192–198; Sensations 182–186

Expansion-Contraction 35, 120, 177, 179

Falling 182–186

Fantasize, Do, Radiate (FDR) 2

Fantastic Action 190–191

fantasy/fantasizing 2, 17, 125, 129, 164, 188

FDR *see* Fantasize, Do, Radiate

Feeling Center 187, 188, 189

First Lord 63–64

Flowing 176–178, 186

Flying 176–178

form 2, 6, 9, 174, 180, 186

Gertrude 85–86

Gil, Eva 176

Goneril 88–89

204 INDEX

Great Lakes Michael Chekhov Consortium (GLMCC) 2, 174

Hamlet (character in *Hamlet*) 173
*Hamlet:* monologues 82–83, 85–86, 100–102; soliloquy 83–84
Helena *(All's Well That Ends Well)* 167–169
Helena *(Midsummer Night's Dream)* 49–51
*Henry IV, Part I* 139–141
*Henry IV, Part II:* monologues 121–122, 142–144; soliloquy 141–142
*Henry V:* monologue 144–147; soliloquy 122–124
*Henry VI, Part I* 124–125
*Henry VI, Part II* 125–128
*Henry VI, Part III* 128–129
Hermione 157–159
Higher Ego 178
histories (Shakespeare): men 131–154; women 119–131
Hotspur 139–141

Iachimo 160–162
Iago 110–111
iambic pentameter 31
Imaginary Body: and Archetype 33, 37; exercises 174–175
Imagination: exercises 174–191; in monologues 147; in sonnets 9, 17
Imogen 156–157, 162
in class/rehearsal exercises: Imaginary Body 174–175; Psychological Gesture 178–180; Qualities of Movement 176–178; Subjective/Objective Atmosphere 180–182
Individual Feelings 3

Inspired Acting 17
Isabella 169–170, 173

Jacques 192–193
Jewelry 33, 37
Joan de Pucelle 124–125
John of Gaunt 131–133
Julia 57–61
Juliet 94–96
*Julius Caesar:* monologues 86–88, 102–105; soliloquy 105–106

King Edward IV *(Richard III)* 152–154
King Henry IV *(Henry IV, Part II)* 141–142
King Henry V 144–147
*King Lear:* monologue 88–89; soliloquy 107–108
King Richard *(Richard II)* 133–137
King Richard *(Richard III)* 148–152
Koeth, Jamie 191

Lady Anne 130–131
Lady Macbeth 90–93
Lady Percy 121–122
Launce 75–77
Launcelot Gobbo 67–69
Laws of Composition 4, 149, 152
Life-Body 183–184, 186–191
*Love's Labour's Lost* 64–66
Lower Self 178
Luciana 40–42
Lysander 69–70

Macbeth (character in Macbeth) 109–110
*Macbeth* 90–91, 109–110
*Measure for Measure* 169–170, 172–173

INDEX    205

*Merchant of Venice, The:* monologues
43–47, 66–67; soliloquy 67–69
Merlin, Joanna 181, 185
Michael Chekhov
   Technique: approach to
   character 32–33; 'expansion
   and contraction' 120; and
   imagination 17; 'inner-
   outer' tempo 111; Laws of
   Composition 4, 149, 152;
   Radiating 183; and scoring
   184–185; Sensations 183, 186;
   tools 1–6; 'veiling' 53
*Midsummer Night's Dream,*
   *A:* monologues 32, 47–49, 69–70,
   197–198; soliloquies 49–51,
   70–71
Molding 176–178
monologues: *As You Like It* 32,
   33–40, 61–64, 192–193; *Antony
   and Cleopatra* 79–82, 96–98;
   *Comedy of Errors, The* 40–42,
   195–198; *Coriolanus* 98–100;
   *Cymbeline* 160–162; exercises
   184–186, 188–190, 192–198;
   *Hamlet* 82–83, 85–86, 100–102;
   *Henry IV, Part I* 139–141; *Henry
   IV, Part II* 121–122, 142–144;
   *Henry V* 144–147; *Henry VI,
   Part I* 124–125; *Henry VI, Part
   II* 125–128; *Henry VI, Part
   III* 128–129; *Julius Caesar* 86–88,
   102–105; *King Lear* 88–89;
   *Love's Labour's Lost* 64–66;
   *Macbeth* 91–93; *Measure for
   Measure* 169–170, 172–173;
   *Merchant of Venice, The* 43–47,
   66–67; *Midsummer Night's Dream,
   A* 47–49, 51–53, 69–70, 197–198;
   *Much Ado About Nothing* 193–195;

*Othello* 93–94, 110–111;
   *Richard II* 119–120, 131–139;
   *Richard III* 130–131, 152–154;
   *Romeo and Juliet* 111–113;
   *Tempest, The* 163–167; *Titus
   Andronicus* 113–116; *Troilus
   and Cressida* 170–171; *Twelfth
   Night* 55–57, 73–75; *Winter's Tale,
   The* 157–160
mood 3
*Much Ado About Nothing:* monologue
   193–195; soliloquy 71–73
Myss, Caroline 2

OB *see* Objective
Objective (OB): definition 5;
   soliloquies 108; sonnets 31
Objective Atmosphere 3
Obstacles (OS): definition 5
Olivia 55–57
*On the Technique of
   Acting* (Chekhov) 181
operative words 31, 42
Ophelia 82–84
Orsino 73–75
OS *see* Obstacles
*Othello* 93–94, 110–111

Paulina 159–160
Perrone, Nicole 180
Petit, Lenard 2, 186
PG *see* Psychological Gesture
Phoebe 33–37, 125
pitch 134, 136, 138, 159
PL *see* Polarity
Polarity (PL) 5; exercises 186; in
   monologues 53, 83, 89, 113, 126; in
   soliloquies 69, 152; in sonnets 13
Polonius 100–102
Portia (*Julius Caesar*) 86–87

Portia (*Merchant of Venice*) 43–47
Prince Hal 142–144
problem plays: men 172–173;
    women 167–171
Prospero 165–167
Psycho-Physical Action 4–5
psycho-physical exercises
    182–186, 190
Psychological Gesture (PG)
    2; definition 5–6; exercises
    178–180, 183, 191
Puck 197–198
punctuation 31, 69, 134, 147

QA *see* Quality of Action
QoM *see* Qualities of Movement
Qualities of Movement (QoM):
    exercises 176–178, 183
Quality of Action (QA) 2; definition
    5; exercises 190; in sonnets 30–31
Queen Margaret (*Henry VI, Part II*)
    125–126
Queen Margaret (*Henry VI, Part III*)
    128–129

Radiation/Radiating 103, 124, 141,
    176–178, 183–184, 186–188
rehearsal: climaxes 4; soliloquies
    124; sonnets 9; speeches 98,
    139; *see also* in class/rehearsal
    exercises
rhyming couplets 13, 16, 17, 42
rhythm: group 177; soliloquies 106;
    sonnets 7, 13, 31
Rhythmical Wave (RW) 4, 5; *As You
    Like It* 37; audience and 31, 141;
    definition 6; *Julius Caesar* 106;
    *Midsummer Night's Dream, A* 69;
    *Richard III* 152; sonnets 13, 31; in
    speeches 33

*Richard II* 119–120, 131–139
*Richard III:* monologues 130–131,
    152–154; soliloquies 148–152
Rising 182–186
romances (Shakespeare): men
    160–167; women 156–160
Romeo 111–113
*Romeo and Juliet:* monologue
    111–113; soliloquy 94–96
Rosalind 37–40

scansion 31, 93
scoring 18, 31, 198–198
self 32
Sensations: application to
    monologue work 184–186;
    exercises 182–186
Shakespeare, William: comedies
    32–78, 192–198; histories
    119–154; 'pants' roles 40,
    157; problem plays 167–173;
    romances 156–167; sonnets
    7–31; speaking through Prospero
    166; speeches 32–33; tragedies
    79–116; use of archetypes 33
Shylock 66–67
Smith, Leah 191
soliloquies: *All's Well That Ends Well*
    167–169; audience involvement
    23, 49; *Cymbeline* 156–157;
    *Hamlet* 83–84; *Henry IV, Part
    II* 141–142; *Henry V* 122–124;
    *Julius Caesar* 105–106; *King
    Lear* 107–108; *Macbeth* 90–91,
    109–110; *Midsummer Night's
    Dream, A* 49–51, 70–71; *Much
    Ado About Nothing* 71–73; rhythm
    106; *Richard III* 148–152; *Romeo
    and Juliet* 94–96; *Two Gentlemen of
    Verona, The* 57–61, 75–77

# INDEX

sonnets 7–31; Action and Quality of Action 30–31; Archetypes 31; Artistic Frame 31; audience involvement 23; as audition pieces 7, 30–31; breath 31; character and characterization 7, 9, 31; climax 31; form 9; Imagination 17; operative words 31; personalization 22; Polarity 13; punctuation 31; Rhythmical Wave 7, 13, 31; scansion 31; tempo/rhythm 7, 31; vocal range 31; volume 31

ST *see* Stakes

Stakes (ST): definition 5; monologues 125; soliloquies 142

Stanislavski, Konstantin 2

Subjective/Objective Atmosphere exercise 180–182

tactics *see* Action

*Tempest, The* 163–167

tempo: exercises 178, 181; inner and outer 4, 67, 111, 147, 170; monologues 37, 67, 98, 116, 122, 140–141, 146, 147, 170; and Rhythmical Wave 6; soliloquies 106, 110, 124; sonnets 7, 14, 22, 31

Titania 32, 51–53

Titus 113–114

*Titus Andronicus* 113–116

*To the Actor* (Chekhov) 4, 174, 176

Touchstone 32

tragedies (Shakespeare): men 96–116; women 79–96

Trinculo 163–164

*Troilus and Cressida* 170–171

truth 2

Tuttle, Jennifer 178

*Twelfth Night:* monologues 55–57, 73–75; soliloquy 53–55

*Two Gentlemen of Verona, The* 57–61, 75–77

type casting 33

Veiling 73, 135, 148, 150

Viola 53–55

vocal range 31

volume 31, 124, 138, 159

Walsh, Lionel 186

*Winter's Tale, The* 157–160

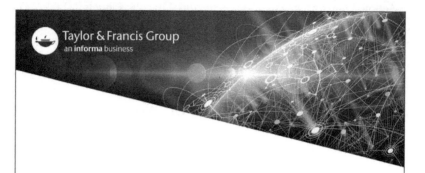